STORIES FROM THE BOW SEAT

THE WISDOM & WAGGERY OF CANOE TRIPPING

STORIES FROM THE BOW SEAT

THE WISDOM & WAGGERY OF CANOE TRIPPING

DON STANDFIELD AND LIZ LUNDELL

The BOSTON
MILLS PRESS

To the memory of O. R. Lundell,
and for Carolyn, Win, and Jim,
with love and gratitude

Canadian Cataloguing in Publication Data

Standfield, Don 1955–
Stories from the bow seat: the wisdom and waggery of canoe tripping

ISBN 1-55046-188-5

1. Canoes and canoeing - Canada - History. 2. Canoes and canoeing - Canada - History - Pictorial works. 3. Canoes and canoeing - United States - History. 4. Canoes and canoeing - United States - History - Pictorial works. I. Lundell, Liz—   . II. Title I. Title.

GV776.15.A2S72 1999   797.1'22'0971   C99-931904-3

03 02 01 00 99   1 2 3 4 5

Published in 1999 by
BOSTON MILLS PRESS
132 Main Street
Erin, Ontario N0B 1T0
Tel 519-833-2407
Fax 519-833-2195
e-mail books@boston-mills.on.ca
www.boston-mills.on.ca

Distributed in Canada by
General Distribution Services Limited
325 Humber College Boulevard
Toronto, Canada M9W 7C3
Orders 1-800-387-0141 Ontario & Quebec
Orders 1-800-387-0172 NW Ontario & Other Provinces
e-mail customer.service@ccmailgw.genpub.com
EDI Canadian Telebook S1150391

Distributed in the United States by
General Distribution Services Inc.
85 River Rock Drive, Suite 202
Buffalo, New York 14207-2170
Toll-free 1-800-805-1083
Toll-free fax 1-800-481-6207
e-mail gdsinc@genpub.com
www.genpub.com
PUBNET 6307949

We acknowledge for their financial support of our publishing program the Canada Council, the Ontario Arts Council, and the Government of Canada through the Book Publishing Industry Development Program (BPIDP).

THE CANADA COUNCIL | LE CONSEIL DES ARTS
FOR THE ARTS | DU CANADA
SINCE 1957 | DEPUIS 1957

This book is endorsed by the Canadian Recreational Canoeing Association. Founded in 1971, the CRCA is dedicated to increasing worldwide knowledge of Canadian paddling activities, to providing canoe, kayak and sea kayak route information, and to lobbying for appropriate environmental conservation.

Canadian Recreational Canoeing Association,
P.O. Box 398, 446 Main Street West, Merrickville, Ontario, Canada K0G 1N0
Tel 613-269-2910 Fax 613-269-2908 www.crca.ca staff@crca.ca
To subscribe to the CRCA's quarterly publication,
Kanawa magazine, phone toll-free 1-888-252-6292.

Design by Gillian Stead
Printed in Hong Kong by
Book Art Inc., Toronto

CONTENTS

INTRODUCTION

Our Route

We lashed the canoes together loosely with two deadfalls and a few lengths of yellow rope. The tarp, raised between two paddles, ballooned across the bows and I ruddered lightly in the stern to keep our course. The others chatted in lulling tones, leaning back against the sun-warmed packs. Clouds drifted across the perfect blue, while water and wind strummed silvery tones along the canoes. Two trolling lines trailed behind us and soon we felt tugs on both. Out came the stove, the frying pan, and flour, and within minutes we were passing forks and a panful of golden lake trout filets. Later that bug-free night, when the fire had burned down, we stretched out on the sloping granite and watched northern lights ripple in rings of scarlet and emerald.

At times like these, the canoe-trip stories flow. They drift from one to the next, forming a collage of other moments, of complete peace, of proud achievements, and even failures — memories of the buggiest portage, the tastiest meal, the worst storm, or the most terrifying rapids. The appeal of canoe journeys shines through, sparked by newcomers' observations and fueled by the long-burning memories of seasoned paddlers. Some of the stories are full of compelling detail; the smoke of many fires softens others. Each adds to the warmth and intensity of our shared experience.

The book in front of you is a collection of similar canoe-trip impressions, the types of stories you might hear while relaxing in the bow of a canoe or around a campfire.

ILLUSTRATION BY F. S. COBURN, CIRCA 1900.

Canoe Manned by Voyageurs
Passing a Waterfall.
FRANCES ANNE HOPKINS, 1869

Bona fide Shangri-La.
Heading deeper into the Fraser Fiord.

Before setting out on any canoe trip, the route options are limitless. Maps tumble across the table and floor, wide expanses of blue and green beckon. Memories of past trips and hints from other trippers pique interest in any number of waterways or directions. There comes a point, though, when we narrow the field and select one route; others will have to wait for other seasons.

The directions we could have followed in putting together this collection were similarly infinite. There are as many individual impressions, stories, and experiences of canoe trips as there are blackflies on a spring day. Only a fraction could be included. The rest await telling around some other campfire.

So what are these *Stories from the Bow Seat*? They are descriptions of canoe trips of the past four hundred years or so that have touched most of the wild canoe areas in North America. Some are beautifully worded wisdom on the essence of canoe travel, others are grippingly descriptive, and still others are pure waggery. They are told by trippers from different eras, and of various ages, interests, and abilities. Some are old salts experienced in wilderness guiding, while others see canoe tripping through the fresh eyes of a novice.

Many selections acknowledge the gift that canoe travelers received from the First Nations people who developed and shared what the legendary Bill Mason called "the most beautiful and functional object that humanity has ever created." A sense of respect and appreciation for those people who first marked out portages, traveled the water routes, and who shared the skills required to travel in the wilderness comes through in these images and essays. Some of the language in the older excerpts reflects a historical era and social milieu different from our own. We must bear this in mind when we encounter the exclusive use of "men" to refer to canoe travelers, or certain Eurocentric labels for people of Native descent.

The reasons for canoe travel have also changed over the years. While most of today's canoe trips are recreational, earlier canoe journeys fulfilled quite different purposes. The first inhabitants relied on the canoe

After many years of dedicated canoe-tripping research,
Chris Blythe and Bob Henderson finally disprove the Flat Earth Society.

for transportation and basic sustenance, but canoe journeys also figured in the spiritual life of many First Nations people. Canoe travel was essential to European exploration and to the mapping of this continent. Some adventurers undertook these voyages for the glory of king and country, but more embarked for commercial reasons. Missionary accounts emphasize the faith and forbearance required in facing the trials of canoe travel.

The *coureur de bois* and *voyageurs* of the fur-trade era have become canoeing icons, and trippers today often think back on their legendary exploits while on the trail. Geological surveys and other scientific research prompted many of the canoe trips of the 1800s, while during this century recreation has become the main focus. Improved access by rail and later air, an increasingly urban population seeking escape, and the growth of environmental awareness have all contributed to canoeing's popularity.

The reasons for recounting canoe-trip experiences have also evolved. There are tersely worded progress reports from explorers, detailed descriptions of unfamiliar routes, scientific observations, letters, personal journals, and philosophical introspectives written for personal enjoyment or publication. Styles vary widely, but the canoe travelers often share an understated approach, appreciative of the ironic situations in which they find themselves. Some accounts are completely tongue-in-cheek.

Northwest Canoe on Strathcona River

In spite of differing purposes, historical periods, and approaches, the selections, when taken together, reflect the universal experiences of all who travel by canoe. Many aspects are timeless. The transforming qualities of a canoe trip endure. For this reason, the material does not follow a chronological or even geographical path. The impressions are grouped around the stages of a canoe trip, each illustrating an aspect of what could be seen as a single, collective canoe journey spanning the centuries and the breadth of North America's canoe country.

So put down your paddle and stretch a while. Take a deep breath of smoke-scented calm or wrap your hands around a steaming mug...and get ready to add your own canoe trip stories.

So dat's de reason I drink to-night
To de man of de Grand Nor' Wes',
For hees heart was young,
an' hees heart was light
So long as he's leevin' dere –
I'm proud of de sam' blood in my vein
I'm a son of de Nort' Win' wance again –
So we'll fill her up till de bottle's drain
An' drink to de Voyageur.

FROM "THE VOYAGEUR," HENRY DRUMMOND

Why Go ?

WILDERNESS DISCOVERED

Many years ago, when I was an instructor of English at the University of Vermont, I was friends with the principal of a large high school in the town. He was jolly and full of fun, loved puns and jokes even when the jokes were on himself. Very clever too. One year, Columbus Day came and he had to invent a school play celebrating the discovery of America. I don't know whether you have a Columbus Day holiday in Canada or not, probably not. I always like a story about Columbus: when he started out, he didn't know where he was going. When he got there, he didn't know where he was. And when he got back home, he didn't know where he had been. For this reason he is known as the Great Navigator.

Well, this is the play my friend devised. The curtain rises, disclosing Indians lurking behind trees. They are peering out at a painted screen showing Columbus debarking from his high-sterned vessel into a ship's boat, to be rowed ashore. The Indian chief declaims to his followers, "Now we are discovered!"

Columbus was discovering America and native Americans were discovering Columbus and multitudinous followers, much to their sorrow. Makes you wonder who was discovering whom.

It is a little like that with us and wilderness lakes and rivers. They are new to you and fresh and thrilling. But they've been there a long time. It is really you canoe-and-portage travelers who are new to them. It would be poetic fallacy to assume the wilderness says anything...the great brooding man-less wilderness is just *there*, not caring whether you live or die. It doesn't say anything. And yet, in some magic, unexplainable way, something very much like that happens. Those wild, faraway places inspire you, they make you strong and happy, they teach you, they also force you to become humble, they punish your mistakes, and make you alert and observant and keen to know the ancient arts of survival.

Elliot Merrick, *Nastawgan*

I went along to iron out the wrinkles in my soul.
OMOND SOLANDT

CONNECTIONS

First, the canoe connects us to *Ma-ka-ina*, Mother Earth, from which we came and to which we must all return. Councils of those who were here before us revered the earth and also the wind, the rain, and the sun — all essential for life. It was from that remarkable blending of forces that mankind was allowed to create the canoe and its several kindred forms.

From the birch tree came the bark; from the spruce, the pliant roots; from the cedar, the ribs, planking and gunwales; and from a variety of natural sources, the sealing pitch.

In other habitats, great trees became dugout canoes while, in treeless areas, skin, bone and sinew were ingeniously fused into kayaks. Form followed function, and manufacture was linked to available materials. Even the modern canoe, although several steps away from the first, is still a product of the earth. We have a great debt to those who experienced the land before us. No wonder that, in many parts of the world, the people thank the land for allowing its spirit to be transferred to the canoe.

Hand-propelled watercraft still allow us to pursue that elemental quest for tranquillity, beauty, peace, freedom and cleanness. It is good to be conveyed quietly, gracefully, to natural rhythms. . . .

The canoe especially connects us to rivers — timeless pathways of the wilderness. Wave after wave of users have passed by. Gentle rains falling onto a paddler evaporate skyward to form clouds and then to descend on a fellow traveller, perhaps in another era. Likewise, our waterways contain something of the substance of our ancestors. The canoe connects us to the spirit of these people who walk beside us as we glide silently along riverine trails.

Kirk Wipper, in *Canexus*

ADVENTURE AND RISK

Yet accidents can happen even to expert canoeists. Gino Watkins, the brilliant young English explorer, died while seal hunting on an expedition to Greenland in 1932. He had been kayaking alone. His kayak was found floating in the water and his clothes were lying on an ice floe, but his body was never recovered. He had been as skilled as the Eskimos in seal hunting, but even the Eskimos rarely hunt alone. Cautious explorers minimize risks. Vilhjalmur Stefansson, whose explorations were even more impressive than Watkins', felt that "having an adventure is a sign that something unexpected, something unprovided against, has happened; it shows that someone is incompetent, that something has gone wrong."

Blair Fraser died in a canoeing accident on the Rollway Rapids of the Petawawa River in May 1968. He was with a group of the "Voyageurs," all experienced canoeists who, since 1951, had in innumerable trips covered thousands of miles of Canadian wilderness, including much river canoeing. Fraser and his canoeing partner missed the takeout for the portage; the canoe shipped water and sank in the first few standing waves. His partner survived, but Fraser drowned. They were wearing lifejackets, and the party was large enough to be of adequate support. The only factor on the AMC list [Appalachian Mountain Club's List of River Hazards] was cold

spring water. It was the kind of error which no amount of experience or preparation can be guaranteed to avoid....

Some risks are unavoidable in white water canoeing, but the risks tend to be exaggerated because the failures, not the successes, are publicized. Scientists who have studied human desires for, and responses to, high-risk physical activity have found that taking part in these sports produces a state of well-being in the participant which can approach euphoria. The sense of satisfaction and personal competence arising from successfully completing an arduous and challenging canoe trip can last for months and helps put the rest of life in perspective. Meeting and overcoming physical risks is still a basic human need.

In modern western society life has a much higher value than it has in other places, or has had at other times. The hardships endured not only by wilderness explorers but by the average traveller on the major fur trade routes less than a century ago would be unacceptable in Canada in the 1970s [or today]. So also would be the risks of fractures, infections, hernias and drowning the voyageurs faced. Life was cheap, and often short, in those days. Now there is a tendency to condemn physical risk-taking in sports as foolish. But one of the few important certainties in human life is that we are all going to die. Modern medicine has increased the possibility of dying a passive death at the end of a lingering and painful terminal illness. Sports like white water canoeing slightly increase the chances of a quick and active death. Many doctors take up white water canoeing — more in proportion than lawyers, accountants or engineers. Dr. Walt Blackadar, possibly the most adventurous white water canoeist in the world, commented at the beginning of his most dangerous trip: "I'm not suicidal but get depressed watching so many patients with incurable diseases." He and many other people have found that in a strange but powerful way, risk-taking in sport is an affirmation and celebration of life

C.E.S. Franks, *The Canoe and White Water*

After you have exhausted what there is in business, politics, conviviality, and so on – have found that none of these finally satisfy, or permanently wear – what remains? Nature remains.

WALT WHITMAN

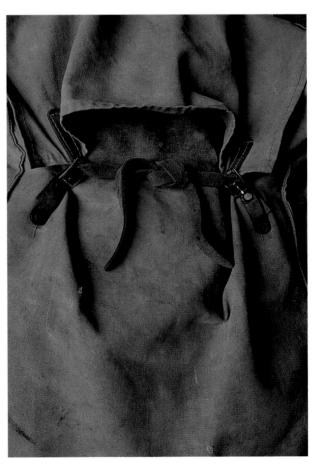

Voyageurs nouvelles return home on the last day of a 50-day trip.

EXHAUSTION AND FULFILMENT: THE ASCETIC IN A CANOE

What sets a canoeing expedition apart is that it purifies you more rapidly and inescapably than any other. Travel 1000 miles by train and you are a brute; pedal 500 miles on a bicycle and you remain basically a bourgeois; paddle 100 miles in a canoe and you are already a child of nature.

For it is a condition of such a trip that you entrust yourself, stripped of your worldly goods, to nature. Canoe and paddle, blanket and knife, salt pork and flour, fishing rod and rifle: that is about the extent of your wealth. To remove all the useless material baggage from a man's heritage, is, at the same time, to free his mind.

On the other hand, what fabulous and undeveloped mines are to be found in nature, friendship and oneself! The paddler has no choice but to draw everything from them. Later, forgetting that this habit was adopted under duress, he will be astonished to find so many resources within himself....

The canoe is also a school of friendship. You learn that your best friend is not a rifle, but someone who shares a night's sleep with you after ten hours of paddling at the other end of a canoe. Let's say that you have to be towed up a rapid and it's your turn to stay in the canoe and guide it. You watch your friend stumbling over logs, sliding on rocks, sticking in gumbo, tearing the skin on his legs and drinking water for which he does not thirst, yet never letting go of the rope; meanwhile, safely in the middle of the cataract, you spray your hauler with a stream of derision. When this same man has also fed you exactly half his catch, and has made a double portage because of your injury, you can boast of having a friend for life.

How does the trip affect your personality? Allow me to make a fine distinction, and I would say that you return not so much a man who reasons more, but a more reasonable man. For, throughout this time, your mind has learned to exercise itself in the working conditions which nature intended. Its primordial role has been to sustain the body in the struggle against a powerful universe. A good camper knows that it is more important to be ingenuous than to be a genius. And conversely, the body, by demonstrating the true meaning of sensual pleasure, has been of service to the mind. You feel the beauty of animal pleasure when you draw a deep breath of rich morning air right through your body, which has been carried by the cold night, curled up like an unborn child. How can you describe the feeling which wells up in the heart and stomach as the canoe finally rides up on the shore of the campsite after a long day of plunging your paddle into rain-swept waters? Purely physical is the joy which the fire spreads through the palms of your hands and the soles of your feet while your mouth belches the poisonous cold.

The pleasurable torpor of such a moment is perhaps not too different from what the mystics of the East are seeking.

Pierre Elliott Trudeau,
in *Jeunesse etudiante catholique*, November 1944,
translated in *Wilderness Canada*

TALKING ABOUT MY REGENERATION

If I don't get away from cars and concrete at least one week a year, I go crazy. I need a minimum of seven days in the woods to feel that summer, so fleeting, has really happened. I need to get out in a canoe.

I discovered this on the long wooden dock at the Portage Store in Algonquin Park in the seventies, where friends took me the year I immigrated to Canada. There was an alchemical moment when we climbed into our rented Grummans and picked up paddles, left engine noise and exhaust behind in the parking lot and entered a clean, silent world where you could fill your lungs with sweet-smelling air and drink the water you floated on. It was spellbinding, irresistible. I was hooked. People didn't go camping in the flat, agricultural lands around my hometown. I'd never even heard of the Canadian Shield, much less dreamed such beauty was accessible.

So began summers of cajoling friends with cars, borrowing tents, aluminum pots, wrapping mountains of oatmeal and Tang in plastic bags. When my canoeing buddies eventually found other interests, I tried professional trips, figuring the leaders would have hot tips on streamlining gear, campfire cooking, etc. — the drudge end of the business. That's when I learned whitewater strokes — the draw, the sweep, the brace — and found I'd been doing the J-stroke backward all those years. Nobody'd ever told me.

Finally I took some trips with naturalists, and at long last discovered the difference between white pines and red, between hermit thrushes and Swainson's; that the haunting "Oh, Canada, Canada, Canada" song in a summer woods is made by the white-throated sparrows. At long last I'd found a key to that exquisite, breathtaking world.

In the eighties I acquired my own canoe, tent, car — in that order. And husband, who was not only a canoeist, but could recognize every bird along the river from its song. My "rivers list" began to read like a dream: Dumoine, Mississagi, Berens, Groundhog, Spanish, Coppermine, Roseberry, Thelon. Best trips were ones volunteering for the *Ontario Breeding Bird Atlas*, where, thanks to project partners, we'd be dropped off by floatplane a hundred miles north of the nearest road and picked up again three weeks later.

In the nineties my husband and I spent a few summer vacations nosing around the continent with canoe on top of car, tent in trunk. It wasn't the

Imagine, if you will, naming the 30,000 islands on Georgian Bay

same. One summer, thanks to frequent-flyer points, we even drove around Australia. Fabulous trip, but it wasn't the same, either. A visit to steamy, sun-scorched India made me vividly aware of how lucky — so darn lucky — we Canadians are with our shade, our water, our solitude. If we could send them just one river, I figured — one clean, splashing, tree-lined stream — it would change the whole subcontinent.

I know our own visits to our beautiful northlands are part of the impact we humans are having, even though we leave only the occasional scrape of paint on a rock, the imprint of our tent among the trees. When humans move in, wildlife often moves on. Paradoxically, I know I need to go there. Nature doesn't just regenerate forests and ecosystems, it regenerates *me*.

Margaret Carney, "I Found It Again in the Buffer Zone"

A small reminder that the White Pine portage into Dog Bite Lake is 4,200 yards of uphill cursing.

I would always carry some brandy for the group on the trips I guided, to get things moving on those frosty mornings or in case of an emergency. You see, if someone cut a foot off with an axe while chopping wood, I could run back to the tent and take a couple of great big swigs of brandy before dealing with the situation.

JIM SPENCER, GUIDE

PUSHING LIMITS

I bet if you took a poll of people who are lifelong trippers and asked them about their first trip as a kid, a lot of them would say, "I really didn't care for it a whole lot."

I remember my first trip like it was yesterday. Eleven years old. Four days. The second portage, the strap on my pack broke. I distinctly remember — and I'm going back 31 years now — sitting on this pack with the broken strap, in the middle of the trail, crying my eyes out and yelling for the headman at the top of my lungs.

He came back, asked me what the problem was, and tied this big knot in the pack. He picked it up and I slithered back into the straps. He walked with me. He didn't carry the pack (there's a great lesson in life there), but he talked to me and kept me from thinking about the agony of this terrible thing I was going through until we made it to the end of the portage.

That first trip stands out so clearly and I remember coming back to camp after that trip and thinking, "If this is what we do at camp all summer, this may not have been the wisest choice." It only clicked on my second trip that this was a real adventure.

"I think," said Christopher Robin, "that we ought
to eat all our provisions now,
so we won't have as much to carry."

A. A. MILNE

And then, we've all had those times on trip when everything just seems to work. You get into the swing of tripping. You've become such a team that you don't have to say anything when you get to a portage. The bowman gets out and straddles, and the middleman takes a pack out with him and sets it on a nice big rock, and everyone helps take the canoe out. It's like a well-oiled machine. It doesn't happen overnight. Some kids never get it, but it's such a kick when that happens.

You have to be a pretty strong character if you're going to be a successful canoe-tripper. And if you're a successful tripper, it sticks with you throughout life. You can learn to make the most of what you have and to live without an awful lot. It's hard to tell a ten-year-old kid this because he doesn't give a hoot about maturity and responsibility and all the things he's going to get out of this. It's all about doing things you didn't think you could do. You learn to push yourself and you begin to realize that there are no such things as limits anymore. And the neatest thing that can happen for any kid is they're going to find something out there on the trail that will keep them coming back.

If you ask any young kid how his first trip went, more often than not, he's going to say it was miserable. When they first get back from trip, they say, "Man, that was tough." They like to talk about the weather, especially if they were wet for six days in a row, about how miserable they were. They also like to talk about the wildlife. Maybe they heard wolves. They love to gripe about the food, which surprises me, because I always remembered when I was a kid that everything tasted good on the trail. But usually after they've dried off, had some hot food, maybe had a nap or read a few comics, it's amazing how quickly they get over the yucky stuff. They gradually get into this pride thing we have at camp. The tougher it is, the more we like it. We like to go places no sane person would go. "Oh, man, you wouldn't believe how bad it was," you're saying with a smile on your face.

Mac Rand is an educator and former director of Camp Pathfinder, one of the oldest children's camps in Canada, established in 1914.

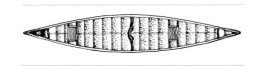

Outfitting and Setting Off

Down the Coppermine with Captain John Franklin in 1819

We gave guns, ammunition, tobacco, blankets and cloth, to the Indians. Our remaining stores were a few unserviceable guns, eight pistols, 24 broad daggers, two barrels of powder, and balls for 2/3 of that quantity, nails and fastenings for a boat, some knives, chisels, files, axes, and a hand saw; six nets, with meshes of different sizes; some cloth, needles, looking glasses, blankets, and beads. Our provision was two barrels of flour, two cases of chocolate, two canisters of tea, 200 dried reindeer tongues, and portable soups, arrowroot, and dried moose meat for ten days. The expedition consisted of 28 persons, including five officers, two interpreters and three Bois brulée women, who were engaged to make shoes and clothes at the winter establishment.

Robert Hood, *To the Arctic by Canoe*

A Maine Packbasket in a Minnesota Canoe

Some years ago I took a Maine packbasket on a Minnesota canoe trip. It was a handsome basket made for me by an Indian and I used it many years. To my surprise, Minnesota canoemen directed endless ribbing at my "clothes basket" and refused to concede that it might be a suitable rig on canoe trails. The only pack, they insisted, was the Duluth, also known as the Northwestern or Poirier. This is, in effect, a large square pocket of canvas, sewn flat with bellows at the side, and equipped with shoulder straps and a tumpline. Its advantages were quickly apparent to me. I returned with one to Maine, where canoemen allowed that it was a "nice pack" but "couldn't hold a candle to a packbasket." Lo, the geographical point of view.

State-of-Mainers and Minnesotans would do well to examine each other's gear, including packs.

Bill Rivière, *Pole, Paddle and Portage*

TECHNOLOGY AND CHOICES

I think that you and I have to be careful, because as we go on these canoe trips we tend to bring along more and more technology, and sometimes we just take it without deciding to make a choice whether to have it or not. For example, I had to decide whether to get into this GPS [Global Positioning Satellite] business or not [for a sixteen-week canoe trip on the Back and Coppermine Rivers in the summer of 1996]. I've decided I'm going to stay away from that one completely because, I think, in a sense, it transforms the wilderness surroundings into a television screen with coordinates on it. And I don't want that.

George Luste, "The Tradition of Wilderness Travel"

Here you find mice
You find snake
You find everything that keeps a soul
awake
But it is shelter
It is home
And it is here you will never feel alone

GRAFFITI ON CABIN WALL

Natives drew their maps based on time, not distance —
so the rivers were short, the lakes long.
It's really a far more practical approach for canoeists.

MICHAEL PEAKE

TO TRAVEL FAST, ONE MUST TRAVEL LIGHT

The customs inspector who examined my belongings in their stout pack-sack did not have a very tiring search. There was my feather sleeping bag, a light eight-pound one; my ax, secured at Ile à la Crosse — it had been manufactured prior to the year 1811 and was very serviceable; a copper tea pail of unknown age; two shirts, one with the tail badly scorched; a medical kit consisting of a small bottle of iodine done up in adhesive tape, and surgical needles; a seven-by-nine piece of balloon silk, which I used as a tent and canoe sail; some twine, nails, trolling hooks, moccasins; a collapsible frying pan and spoon; a jack-knife; and, of infinite importance, a heavy soft leather strap with a broad head band called the "tump-line," by which all one's belongings are carried.

The outfit may appear boastfully small and inadequate, but it was the result of much hard discipline in previous years. The North is vast; distances are great. To travel at all, one must travel fast. To travel fast, one must travel light.

P. G. Downes, 1939
Downes' account *Sleeping Island:
Trip from Pelican Narrows, Saskatchewan
to Nueltin Lake Post, NWT*
was published in 1943.

Duct tape is most decidedly something you do not want to be without.

PETER WOOD, *RUNNING THE RIVERS OF NORTH AMERICA*

canoe: a light, narrow boat that is usually propelled by paddling.

RUNNING LOW ON A PRECIOUS COMMODITY

By now a crisis had hit one canoe-team. Jim Matthews suffers from hay fever, and the pine-tree pollen had been causing him trouble all the way. After exhausting his supply of handkerchiefs and tissues, he had turned to toilet paper, and finally run through all his own and that of his partner, Johnny Davis. The crisis had been hastened by the fact that both of them were rather lavish in their use of this important commodity. The rest of us put on a show of heartlessness in their plight, charging them with profligacy. Toilet paper became precious currency, to be bartered for. A plea for help from John Bayly, portaging a canoe, to get a blackfly out of his eye, was answered by Jim only at the price of ten sheets of toilet paper. Hard bargaining was the order of the day, but neither Jim nor Johnny could bring themselves to barter away their evening daiquiris, though there were several offers.

Eric Morse, *Freshwater Saga*

CEDAR-CANVAS AND COFFEE AT THE HURLEY CANOE WORKS

AN INTERVIEW WITH CANOE-BUILDERS JIM SPENCER AND JACK HURLEY

I got out of the car and heard howling. A beautiful chorus of wild harmonies drifting through the trees and coming from the sled dogs next door. Then came the clang of tack hammers from inside the shop, pounding rhythms that created a natural accompaniment to the primal songs of those furry creatures. I opened the door and was confronted by a tough little beagle with a wagging tail. It was Lou the Shop Dog.

The shop was a Molly Maid's nightmare, but full of history and future fertility. Canoe molds were along one wall, and a variety of canoes, in assorted stages of birth, were sitting in different areas of the shop. Tools were on the bench, off the bench, and under the bench. Sawdust and shavings provided a cushioned floor as I weaved through the planers and saws to the back of the shop, where a sixteen-footer was being planked. The walls were filled with the faces of hundreds of people, ranging from Marilyn Monroe to Jackie Kennedy to Ernest Hemingway to Andy Warhol, but the large majority were related in some way or other to the outdoors and Algonquin Park. Canoe-builders, park rangers, guides, pilots, biologists, tripping partners, and family all hung with a thin veil of cedar dust covering their faces. (If you can identify all the people who are tacked and taped to the shop walls, the Hurley Canoe Works will build you a complimentary canoe.)

We left the singing of Patsy Cline behind for a quiet talk around the kitchen table in Jack's house, just a hammer throw away. The wood stove was humming and we sat down, with a round of refreshments, to discuss the character of the wood-canvas canoe and the philosophies of these two builders who love the smell of steamed cedar in the morning.

STANDFIELD: How did the two of you become canoe-builders and are there times when you question the notion of making a living building the cedar-canvas canoe?

JACK HURLEY: I started doing repairs and recanvassing the fleet of wood-canvas canoes that the Algonquin Outfitters used as rentals in the early seventies. All the rentals back then were the canvas-covered canoes and needed work after some of those trips. I was tutored more or less by Clarence Bogues, who was an old canoemaker in the area.

JIM SPENCER: When I was working at the Oufitters my primary position was as guide, but I was truly head-over-heals in love with the wood-canvas canoe and befriended Clarence. When I came off trip I would spend most of my time in the shop learning all the little tricks and procedures. I became thoroughly intrigued with the process of bending ribs, planking, tacking and the "finishing" of a canoe.

HURLEY: We love what we do and totally believe in the product we create, but I suppose there are times when we scratch our heads. I thought everyone wondered about those things in any job? Please don't tell me that we're the only two little guys out there questioning the meaning of life and the price of tacks.

Q: Couldn't you earn a faster dollar if you started making fiberglass canoes?

HURLEY: Oh, my gawd, you said the "F" word!
SPENCER: We were both raised on the wood-canvas canoe. My first vivid recollection of my mother was when I was sitting on the worn ribs of a wood-canvas canoe and I watched her paddle as we skimmed across the lake and into the mist. I believe in its simple design and the natural materials that it is made from. I also feel a real sense of importance in this type of canoe for historical reasons and its rich "spiritual" value for today's fast-paced society. I never knew of any other type of canoe growing up, and I'm going to be buried in one when I reach the final portage.

HURLEY: Going down a river or crossing a lake in anything but wood-canvas is like floating on a linoleum rug. That's just how it looks when you glance inside one of those types of canoes and watch the bottom flex and shimmer with the water. Whereas, in any wood-canvas canoe you have all these beautiful rich colors of the cedar planking and ribs, hardwood gunwales and decks, and caned seats. Even the smells are nice and directly relate to the environment you are traveling through.

Q: Do you think a cedar-canvas canoe is better suited for travel in the bush?

SPENCER: I suppose there would always be an argument for the different types of materials and canoe designs, but the wood-canvas canoe is one generation away from the birchbark canoe and was made for working and transporting people through the wilderness. It was designed and made out of materials that would stand up to miles and miles of flatwater and whitewater and portaging through very rugged and unexplored terrain. As a trip leader with kids and adults, I have safely traveled across many lakes in a wood-canvas canoe in conditions where other experienced paddlers in a the new-design boats were either windbound or took on water during the crossings.

HURLEY: Paddlers can also repair the canvas canoes in the bush while they travel. In the good 'ol days the natives, voyageurs, and early exploration trips could repair the bark canoes or make entirely new ones out of their surroundings if they destroyed them in a set of rapids. The birchbark and the cedar-canvas canoe and the landscape are in harmony with each other. I suppose, though, things might have been different back in the early days if the paddlers and canoemakers had been able to

Jim Spencer, Lou the Shop Dog, and Jack Hurley

identify the plastic trees. Imagine the beautiful paintings that Frances Hopkins could have done of the voyageurs paddling beat-up aluminum or Kevlar canoes.

SPENCER: That's right. The painting *Canoe Party around Campfire,* showing voyageurs repairing the canoe with birchbark and pitch, could have depicted some burly paddler thumping away at a tin boat with a hammer or using up the last roll of duct tape on a Kevlar.

Q: How important is the bush to the two of you? Is there still a need to get out there and away from the shop?

INTERVIEWED BY DON STANDFIELD
IN MARCH 1997

SPENCER: A canoe trip brings together so many things that makes sense. Regardless of the weather or swarms of bugs, it enables us to understand more about ourselves because of the real-life challenges that confront us out on the trail.

HURLEY: A canoe trip is one of the best ways to leave the technology and fast pace behind. I enjoy traveling through the bush using the traditional methods and equipment that have proven themselves for hundreds of years — the canvas pack, the wanigan, the wooden canoe, and the tumpline. A simple piece of leather stretched across the forehead is still one of the most effective pieces of equipment used by wilderness travelers. Developed by the natives years and years ago, the tump makes it easier to carry the pack, wanigan or canoe. I'm sure this is how the voyageurs carried the loads they did. Then again, those guys were animals, but they used the tumpline exclusively, and for good reason — it worked.

SPENCER: I enjoy the squeak of the leather when the tummy-knots stretch on the wanigan or rub on the thwart of the canoe when you're portaging. It becomes a repetitive with every step and creates a meditative rhythm for the carrier. I think we should talk about the mysterious values of this piece of leather and the subsequent development of neck muscles that women find irresistible.

Q: How would you guys describe your canoe shop?

HURLEY: I think when a customer first walks in, there might be a tendency to perceive a little bit of chaos, but then they recognize history all around them. It's a craft that has been done for hundreds of years, and Jim and I are basically

using the same woods and doing the same procedures that create the same smells, the same noises, and the same beautiful canoe that was built generations ago. The shop is full of wonderful smells, and in the winter it's phenomenal.

Q: Why do the cedar-canvas canoe-builders put so much effort into each canoe? There must be lots of ways that would save time and still enable you to create a respectable canoe.

SPENCER: I think we all like to build a canoe that lives up to its original genius. Jack and I spend about seventy hours on a canoe and would rather spend too much time than not enough. Even the early builders of birchbark canoes put thought and time into the design and created beautiful entry lines with protruding stempieces and headboards. The importance of detail was demonstrated in the methodical lashing of spruce roots and the bark-skin itself. The inside of the birchbark became the outside of the canoe, and the rind enabled people to scrape elaborate designs at both ends and along the length of the canoe below the outside gunwale. Each canoe expressed the pride of its builder and reflected in its paddlers.

Q: After all these years of making canoes do you have any horror stories?

SPENCER: Actually most of the tense moments are associated with painting. There was one occasion when Jack was painting a canoe and the people who had ordered it unexpectedly arrived at the shop and inquired what stage we were at or indeed had we finished their canoe. I was happy to tell them that it was completed and we walked over to where Jack was painting it. We all stood there admiring this beautiful beast and watched Jack generously apply the

paint so that the customer could see the canvas really being covered. It looked impressive and they stated that we had done a really fine job, but that they wanted their canoe painted green and not the bright red that was being smothered into the canvas. The comment took me completely off-guard and I had no idea what to say, but Jack, without missing a stroke with the paintbrush, told them not to worry about the color because this red paint was just the primer. When they left I gave Jack a few good pats on the back, and we decided it was definitely cause for ceremony and celebration. We put the brushes away and popped a couple of cold ones.

Q: Would that happen to be your secret canoe filler sitting over there on the counter?

HURLEY: Yes, that certainly is the filler of choice at this shop. Huge quantities of sour cream are spread into the canvas pores of each canoe.

SPENCER: And we add just a pinch of garlic for our special customers.

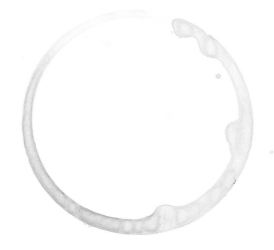

WANIGANS

Wanigan (wonʼəgən) n. Cdn. From the Algonquian *waniigan*, trap, container for stray items. They were the reserve of the seasoned trippers at the summer camp I attended, conferring status on those initiated into the curious rituals of tump-tying. We knew they were of the North, and the trips equipped with them were bound for more exotic, northern destinations with names like Nipigon, Chibougamau, Mattagami.

It wasn't until I went to Temagami that I realized wanigans had been widely used there for ages. We ran into lots of groups carrying versions of the knee-high box, measured to fit into a canoe and rigged with a tumpline for the portages. Some of the wanigans we saw were elaborately outfitted with compartments and spice racks, but the simpler plywood or pine-board boxes worked just as well. It was easy to pack, and a wanigan always protected its cargo, even if it came crashing down accidentally at the end of a portage. One trip, our canoe swamped while we were lining a set of rapids. The box bobbed

Have you never heard of Pandora's wanigan?

gently along until it was thrown up against a slab of granite. When we pulled off the lid and poured out a couple of liters of water, our fresh eggs were still intact. A wanigan also makes a great kitchen table. It's ideal for kneading dough, and there's no risk of a misstep scattering dinner through the dirt and pine needles.

Only once did a wanigan let me down. Although all of our food was hanging in a pack from a tree, the virtually indestructible box must have been sporting a whiff of eau de salami from lunch. I jolted awake from my nap to the sight of a bear derriere outside the tent door. The bear made kindling of the wanigan with one swipe. Then, finding only pots, soap, and a first-aid kit inside it, he lumbered off in disgust. At least the backgammon board we had drawn on the underside of the lid was still functional.

Liz Lundell

STEAMED CEDAR WITH CANVAS

An elegant accompaniment to fish.

Make ahead of time for a relaxed visit with friends.

51	board feet of peeled and deveined eastern white cedar
10	board feet of combined ash, black cherry, and maple
2600	brass tacks
18	feet of 10 weight canvas
3/4	gallon of oil base filler
3	quarts varnish
2	quarts of paint
	Assortment of beers to taste (chilled if possible)

Emile Danderhope's ribs were once considered the best east of the Missippippi.

Using a large shop, prepare all ingredients the night before. Early the next day preheat element to high heat. Bring an adequate quantity of water in a large pot to a tumbling boil. Steam ribs until al dente (flexible) and bend immediately while still tender. Let stand at room temperature to blend flavors until cool. Chop cleaned white parts of planking into long thin slices, (smaller pieces will fall to ground). Add bulk of brass tacks and planks at random until ribs disappear (careful not to tenderize planking with pounding of tacks). When ingredients become solid remove from mold and set aside. Prepare gunwales and decks by chopping fresh hardwoods. Snip to length and desired shape, introducing slowly for best results. Wrap with canvas skin; skewer with tacks along edges, leave middle open. Add both caned seats and center thwart until balanced. Inlay decks for garnish.

Use the same basic recipe for fifteen and seventeen footers. Quantities will vary including concentrations of beer.

Well before serving time, press filler firmly onto bottom side of prepared carcass to seal in natural juices and let marinate. Heat entire hull at medium to high sun for about three weeks, covering occasionally, until fully baked. From a separate pot, baste inside with all-purpose varnish to glaze ribs, careful not to drip, and let harden. Repeat occasionally. Meanwhile, whisk and gently combine, until mixed but not runny, an assortment of fresh paint for color, stirring occasionally as you serve, and dressing the outside lightly from end to end. The condiments blend even better if allowed to stand at medium sun for several hours until sticky topping hardens. (Careful not to undercook, but do not let baking temperature bubble surface.) Repeat spreading of additional layers on outer crust and again set aside and let stand until hard. Cover and place in a safe spot until needed. Present whole at room temperature, arranged attractively on an adequate bed of water. If desired, garnish with cherry paddles as a starter. Bon voyage.
Serves 2 to 3. (Note: Depending on degree of festivities, presentation may be turned into a dip.)

Don Standfield

SIMPLICITY and SPIRITUALITY

from an interview with Esther Keyser,
age 84

*Traveling down to the end of the lake, through
curtains of mist and a brigade of loons, you
arrive at Esther's summer home along a quiet
shoreline tucked underneath several old-growth
white pines. The interior of the cabin is an
extension of the wilderness outside, full of
natural artifacts, antlers and artwork depicting
her love of life within the woods. Still with no
running water or electricity and a wood stove
to keep the chill out of the air, the cabin was
built by Esther in 1937 as a base camp for her
canoe-trip guiding business, which she had
started three years earlier at the age of nineteen.*

I don't think I can explain why I go into
the bush. It's just an urge in me — like
the geese must feel when they head
North. Freedom. Utter freedom. I'm
happier out on the trail than any other
place ... and I really don't know why.
Maybe it's the satisfaction of stripping life
down to its simplest form. Anyhow, it gives
me a high such as nothing else does.

My first canoe trip was as a twelve-year-
old camper at Northway in Algonquin
Park. I can remember every portage,

liftover, lake and campsite on that trip, which was paddled more than seventy years ago. The country seemed so rich and I fell in love with this way of life immediately. Something inside of me said, "This is where you belong," and I have continued to this day, at eighty-four years old, to get out on several canoe trips each year.

Guiding throughout Algonquin in those early years was a dream come true. I used the train quite a bit to get the trip up into the interior faster. We would hop into the baggage car with our canoes and packs and watch the landscape drift by. I was the first woman guide in the Park, so a lot of the men guides knew of me and didn't forget who I was. I was terribly motivated and carried the canoe with some heavy loads across many of the longest and toughest portages.

Esther Keyser, age 26.

After several years of guiding I married a wonderful man and, for our honeymoon, Joe and I went from Dog Lake to James Bay by way of the Missinaibi River. We started at Dog Lake and went over the height of land, and back then in 1941 it was four weeks of complete adventure.

I consider those early times to be the good old days, but there have been some great improvements over the years in equipment and clothing that have helped encourage more people to get out onto the lakes and into the bush. When I was guiding, the acceptable clothing for a woman was completely inadequate for being out in the bush. A long dress really wasn't the most convenient thing to be wearing when jumping over beaver dams or starting fires on the campsite. I really wanted to wear pants, but my mother begged me not to and we compromised on culottes [a divided skirt].

They were sloppy and awkward and pretty hard to dry when they got wet, so I soon changed to pants for most of my guiding trips, along with wool shirts, wool socks, and moccasins that could quickly be slipped off if I had to wade into the water. All my clothing was wool, and we only had the one set. We didn't wear shorts and we didn't swim as much as we do now, but I don't remember being excessively hot, even though I was wearing more clothes than trippers do today.

The tents weren't that great, and I often slept under the canoe and would wrap my head in a towel to keep the bug bites at a minimum. Back then it seemed that we all just sort of accepted and suffered with it. I remember being in a swamp up on the Little Nippissing where we all slept out and the bugs were terrible. We didn't have sleeping bags, but usually everyone had one Hudson Bay blanket. I was short enough that I could roll inside it crosswise, ending up with more than one layer. Then I would pin it up with those big blanket pins. We were all wrapped up from head to toe and, I guess, tired enough that we all went to sleep. In those days wood was very plentiful and we made many a bough bed to sleep on and cooked entirely with wood and always used it for warmth. We seemed to be wet quite a bit, but we quickly learned how to dry ourselves out at the end of most days without many complaints. I don't know, it must have been that we didn't mind as much back then. You would always improvise in one way or another to get around the daily challenges. When you did create, or stumble on, some ingenious solution you certainly remembered it for the next time.

Some of the most enjoyable trips were when Joe and I started canoe-tripping with the kids. When the children were too small to walk, I would take one of the big canvas canoe packs, put a Hudson Bay blanket in, and then stuff the child inside. Once they got to a certain age and were pretty steady on their feet, they would walk the portages and carry a small pack. The first pack that my eldest son carried was full of his sister's diapers.

The menu was kept simple. We didn't really have the variety of foods that we do today. In the early days fish were very plentiful in those lakes and it wasn't such an elaborate science as it is today. We all would count on fish for many meals when traveling through the bush. I baked all types of breads using a primitive, but very effective, oven. I would turn my largest billy-pot on its side in front of the fire and place a pie plate filled with the bread dough inside the pot. For breakfast it was usually stewed fruit that had been soaking all night and a hot cereal. And we drank tea — tea around the campfire in the morning and at night, at the end of a long portage, or under a propped-up canoe waiting for the rain to ease up. Lots and lots of tea, all the time.

I am fortunate to have had so many adventures with good friends in the bush. On my canoe trips, I discovered a wonderful secret for staying young: the act of simplifying life, appreciating and making the most out of what is, and feeling spiritually connected to the land. Those discoveries are magical times for all of us who travel in the wilderness. Being able to paddle and portage and live in a landscape that is home to so many miracles and beautiful animals continues to strengthen my belief that we, too, as humans, belong in these surroundings. We have certainly messed-up this wonderful living arrangement, but I feel we all have a genuine devotion to life that will strengthen the interest in the natural world, I hope, for as long as we have the opportunity to paddle and sleep on the bare bones of this incredible planet.

INTERVIEWED BY DON STANDFIELD IN AUGUST 1998

FITTING IN THE ESSENTIALS

"There's no way we're going to get all this stuff into these three boats and still have any freeboard left."

Somebody had to say it. The process of getting onto the water would be incomplete if there wasn't at least one person who had doubts about whether all of the stuff would fit in the available space. It happens on every trip. Even if you cut yourself back to cornmeal mush and pemmican, this problem would still arise, and it has something to do with three universal laws: (1) Packers always find out how much space will be available for storage and then purposely take a little bit more just to show that they can jam it in; (2) Stuff always looks bulkier when it's spread out on the ground; (3) Humans need with them, on journeys, reminders and comforts of home, technological "essentials" to allow them to survive. For Winnebago-ists, "essentials" may include color televisions, microwave ovens and dozens of matching sets of pastel-colored coordinated sportswear. Our "essentials" stopped short of electrical appliances (if you discount battery-powered cameras and tape recorders). Nevertheless, emergency locator transmitter, ultra-light gas stoves and various other necessary consumer products

Dreams
of
Labrador.

added up to a substantial volume of goods. But fundamentally, whether you're in a canoe or a motor-home, the problems are the same. The difference on a wilderness canoe trip is that you cannot simply put the lawn furniture back in the garage if there is no room left. Either you leave it on the tundra, thereby creating a puzzle for future archaeologists, or you take it with you.

Finally, we're all in with nothing left ashore, taking a couple of tentative strokes to make sure the boats are actually floating and not still beached. We're concerned about freeboard, and reach down from the outside gunwale to see how far it is to the waterline.

Norm calls over, "How's our trim?"

"You're a little stern heavy, but what else is new," replies Lorraine, with a sadistic cackle.

In a few hundred strokes we begin to move with the rhythm of the boat, a few hundred more to synchronize with our partners. But the lake is calm and forgiving this afternoon. We laugh. Everything has fitted in and we're still afloat.

James Raffan's *Summer North of Sixty* describes a 700-kilometer trip down the Back and Burnside Rivers to Bathurst Inlet in 1980

TRIPPING NAKED

H elp me stamp out thermodynamic nudity! That's wearing cotton, folks. If you're in cotton, it gets wet, and if the temperature falls below 50 degrees Fahrenheit, you're dead! It's as simple as that. The body cannot keep up with the heat loss allowed by wet cotton at that temperature or colder. For all practical purposes you're as naked as the Emperor with no clothes. Don't think you are really dressed if you're wearing blue jeans, a cotton sweat shirt, or similar garb and you head for the great outdoors. Actually, you're naked. Most hypothermia deaths occur in the temperature range of 30 to 50 degrees Fahrenheit, and it's because people wore cotton and the clothing got wet.

William Forgey, M.D.

CLOTHING LIST, CIRCA 1886

...a pair of strong kip or cowhide boots, with patch bottoms and Hungarian tacks in the soles. The leg must not be long enough to interfere with the free use of the knee-joint. A pair of light gaiters, or moccasins or leather slippers, to put on when round camp; three or four pairs of light woollen socks, a couple of pairs of strong Guernsey drawers and as many shirts of them same material, and two strong cotton ones, a pair of brown duck, and another of woollen pants, one coat and vest and a few coloured cotton handkerchiefs, a hat and towel....

James Dickson, surveyor, *Camping in the Muskoka Region*

ON THE WATER

CATCHING THE RHYTHM

Dig, pull, swing. Dig, pull, swing.

Like a mantra, the repetition of paddling brings on a trance.

The body carries on while the mind is free to wander...

until aching muscles interject.

FUR TRADE BRIGADES

The canoes for the interior set off from Fort William in brigades, those bound for the most distant posts going first. Between each brigade a space of two days is allowed. This is to prevent a second brigade from reaching a carrying place before the first has completed the several trips necessary, back and forth, across the narrow portage....

In calm weather the canoes generally travel at about six miles per hour. To lighten their labours, the men usually sing a simple melody, keeping perfect time to it with their paddles. When they arrive at a rapid, it is the guide's duty to determine whether it should be run with the full load, half load (the other half being carried by land), or not run at all. "It would be astonishing to a European observer," wrote a partner of the North West Company in 1804, "to witness the dexterity with which they manage their canoes in those dangerous rapids, carrying them down like lightning on the surface of the water. The bowman, supported by the steersman, dexterously avoids the stones and shoals which might touch the canoe and dash it to pieces, to the almost certain destruction of all on board. It often baffles their skill, when the water is very high, to avoid plunging in foaming swells on the very brink of the most tremendous precipices, yet, those bold adventurers rather run this risk, for the sake of expedition, than lose a few hours by transporting the cargo over land.

"When they are obliged to stem the current in strong rapids they haul up the canoe with a line, all hands pulling along shore and sometimes wading through the water up to their middle, except one man, who remains in the stern of the canoe, in order to keep it in the proper channel: this part of their duty is always accompanied with much labour."

Eric Ross, *Beyond the River and the Bay*

TRAVELING FREE

Balance is the goal — between sun time and clock time. Whether or not you make the final break and leave your watch behind, you'll wake with the sun, sleep with the dark, eat (listening to what your body tells you) when you're hungry. Even if your natural cycle makes you a night person in the ordinary routine of life, you'll find yourself getting out of the tent while the others sleep and paddling into the misty half-light of a silent predawn, perhaps with the excuse of casting for an unwary breakfast fish — or simply to wait for the sunrise that, except on a canoe trip, you'll rarely see. And you rediscover out here that time is distance — the distance that takes you, paddle stroke by paddle stroke, from one end of a lake to the other, from portage to portage, from bend of river to rapids to evening campsite; and that the watch you may or may not be wearing on your wrist is not your master but a tool, measuring speed and distance as closely as need be, doubling in a pinch as a compass when set against the dawn or noonday sun. You are traveling free, and by a different and more fundamental time.

Robert Mead, *The Canoer's Bible*

ILLUSTRATION BY F. S. COBURN, CIRCA 1900.

NUELTIN LAKE, NWT

For some time a big canoe had been following us and now it began to draw near. As it came abreast, we saw that it contained a heterogeneous assortment of women, babies, girls, and one young boy. All of them, except the babies, were paddling. As it approached it looked like some ridiculous, great water beetle with a hundred scrambling legs. The stern was in the capable hands of a very large powerful woman. How she could paddle! Despite our four-man power they kept alongside. The woman in the stern took great mile-eating, even strokes, keeping her arms rigid and extended and her back absolutely stiff and straight. The whole motion was from the hips, the power of her stroke being in the rhythmic swing of her body. Grinning and laughing, we went along together, sometimes bursting into sprints which would always be returned in kind by the other canoe. One of the women would occasionally take time out to nurse her baby, but then she would pick up the stroke again.

P. G. Downes, *Sleeping Island*, 1943

Stories from the bow-wow seat.
Chuck and his best friend going out for a five-day trip.

Poling a Canoe

It's not surprising that so few canoe owners have learned to pole their craft in fast water — not when you consider that ever since one of the Pilgrim Fathers swiped Squanto's birch-bark canoe and flipped over in Massachusetts Bay, "experts" have been crying: "Never stand up in a canoe!"

Pseudo-experts have wailed this advice for so many years that the general public has come to believe that the ability to remain upright in a canoe is a mysterious gift allotted only to full-blooded Indians in the employ of the Hudson's Bay Company! The truth is, standing in a canoe, properly done, is as safe as the front pew of a church. Moreover, poling is a comparatively easy skill to acquire....

For years, on rivers close to my former home in southern New Hampshire, I'd grudgingly retreated whenever I encountered a set of rapids. I knew that getting through them with a paddle was impossible, particularly upstream, but being thwarted in this manner rankled. The chortling rips seemed to taunt me, and there was always the nagging thought that beyond the rapids lay miles of idyllic waters and riverbanks, coves to explore, deep holes harbouring big trout, alder runs overpopulated with woodcock, big bucks skulking hard-to-reach swamps bordering on the river.

Hudson's Bay Company canoes poling up the Root River, 1905.

I'd tried portaging, of course, and often the carry path was passable. Not infrequently, though, none existed and I ran into a tangle of impenetrable brush. I'd dragged and lined the canoe through several rips but this was not easy and repeatedly produced a bootful of water and sopping britches.

Then, in 1941, I was assigned by the U.S. Border Patrol to Fort Kent, Maine, where there were more canoes than automobiles, the town being the terminus of the famed Allagash and St. John River trips. Here, Willard Jalbert, a fellow patrolman who'd teethed on a canoe thwart, gave me a taste of white water. Wielding a 14-foot ash pole through rough-and-tumble St. John rapids, while I alternatingly cowered and exulted in the bow, Willard explained the basic technique. He was convincing. I could never match his skill, of that I was sure, but I borrowed a 20-foot Skowhegan canoe and a pole. For two months before winter set in, I wobbled up and down quieter stretches of the river, gradually tackling faster and faster rips. There's been a pole in my canoe ever since.

Bill Rivière, *Pole, Paddle and Portage*

It was inspiriting to hear the regular dip of the paddles.

as if they were our fins or flippers, and to realize that we were at length fairly embarked.

HENRY DAVID THOREAU, *CANOEING IN THE WILDERNESS*, 1916

RUNNING THE RAPIDS. FRANCES ANNE HOPKINS, 1879

God grant me the serenity to walk the portages I must,
The courage to run the rapids I can,
And the wisdom to know the difference.

ANONYMOUS

St. Mary's Falls, 1837

The more I looked upon those glancing, dancing rapids, the more resolute I grew to venture myself in the midst of them....

The canoe being ready, I went to the top of the portage, and we launched into the river. It was a small fishing canoe about ten feet long, quite new, and light and elegant and buoyant as a bird on the waters. I reclined on a mat at the bottom, Indian fashion (there are no seats in a genuine Indian canoe) in a minute we were within the verge of the rapids, and down we went with a whirl and a splash! — the white surge leaping around me — over me. The Indian with astonishing dexterity kept the head of the canoe to the breakers, and somehow or other we danced through them. I could see, as I looked over the edge of the canoe, that the passage between the rocks was sometimes not more than two feet in width, and we had to turn sharp angles — a touch of which would have sent us to destruction — all this I could see through the transparent eddying waters, but I can truly say, I had not even a momentary sensation of fear, but rather of giddy, breathless, delicious excitement. I could even admire the beautiful attitude of a fisher, past whom we swept as we came to the bottom. The whole affair, from the moment I entered the canoe till I reached the landing place, occupied seven minutes, and the distance is about three quarters of a mile.

My Indians were enchanted, and when I reached *home*, my good friends were not less delighted at my exploit: they told me I was the first European female who had ever performed it, and assuredly I shall not be the last. I recommend it as an exercise before breakfast. Two glasses of champagne could not have made me more tipsy and self-complacent!

Anna Jameson, *Winter Studies and Summer Rambles in Canada*, 1923

Dumped!

I am an indifferent swimmer, if any, and this was a dangerous eddy, and deep; there were no hand holds to speak of. So, although it rolled and twisted considerably in the cross current, I stayed with the canoe, on the chance that it would float up, as without it I would be a dead loss anyhow; and soon my head broke water again. The attentive concourse on the river bank, who were in nowise disturbed, evidently thinking we were giving an aquatic performance for their benefit to lighten the cares of a heavy day, were highly diverted, until my companion, on my return to the surface, swam ashore, where his condition apprised them of the true state of affairs. In a matter of seconds a canoe was racing towards me, whilst its occupants shouted encouragement. About this time I was in pretty bad shape, having taken much water, and my hold on the canoe was weakening; so I commenced to shout lustily, suggesting speed. To my horror, one of the men suddenly ceased paddling and commenced to laugh.

"Say," said he. "Why don't you stand up?"

And amidst the cheers and shouts of the appreciative assemblage, I stood up in about three feet of water. I had been floating with my legs out ahead of me, and had drifted backwards within a few yards of the shore.

Grey Owl, *The Men of the Last Frontier*, 1936

CANOE WRECK ON RETURN

On our return, about half way up the Black River, we [Thompson and guides Kozdaw and Paddy] came to one of the falls, with a strong rapid both above and below it. We had a carrying place of 200 yards; we then attempted the strong current above the fall; they were to track the canoe up by a line, walking on shore, while I steered it.

When they had proceeded about eighty yards, they came to a birch tree, growing at the edge of the water, and there stood and disputed among themselves on which side of the tree the tracking line should pass. I called to them to go on, they could not hear me for the noise of the fall, I then waved my hand for them to proceed. Meanwhile the current was drifting me out, and, having only one hand to guide the canoe, the Indians standing still, the canoe took a sheer across the current. To prevent the canoe upsetting, I waved my hand to them to let go the line and leave me to my fate, which they obeyed.

I sprang to the bow of the canoe, took out my clasp knife, cut the line from the canoe and put the knife back in my pocket. By this time I was on the head of the fall; all I could do was to place the canoe to go down bow foremost. In an instant the canoe was precipitated down the fall (twelve feet) and buried under the waves. I was struck out of the canoe, and when I arose among the waves the canoe came on me; and buried beneath it, to raise myself, I struck my feet against the rough bottom and came up close to the canoe, which I grasped, and, being now on shoal water, I was able to conduct the canoe to the shore.

My two companions ran down along the beach to my assistance. Nothing remained in the canoe but an axe, a small tent of grey cotton, and my gun; also a pewter basin. When the canoe was hauled on shore, I had to lay down on the rocks, wounded, bruised, and exhausted by my exertions.

Some people can't stand the sound of paddles
banging on an aluminum canoe.
but I have a bigger problem with
the sound of cedar splintering against rocks.
ANONYMOUS

The Indians went down along the shore, and in half an hour's time returned with my box, lined with cork, containing my sextant and a few instruments and papers of the survey, maps, &c., and our three paddles. We had no time to lose; my all was my shirt and a thin linen vest; my companions were in the same condition. We divided the small tent into three pieces to wrap around ourselves, as a defence against the flies in the day, and something to keep us from the cold at night, for the nights are always cold.

On rising from my rocky bed, I perceived much blood at my left foot; on looking at it, I found the flesh of my foot from the heel to near the toes torn away. This was done when I struck my feet against the rough bottom to rise above the waves of the fall of water. A bit of my share of the tent bound to the wound, and thus barefooted I had to walk over the carrying places with their rude stones and banks.

The Indians went to the woods and procured gum of the pines to repair the canoe; when they returned, the question was how to make a fire; we had neither steel nor flint. I pointed to the gun from which we took the flint. I then produced my pocket knife with its steel blade; if I had drawn a ghost out of my pocket it would not more have surprised them.

They whispered to each other, how avaricious a white man must be, who rushing on death takes care of his little knife; this was often related to other Indians, who all made the same remark. I said to them, "If I had not saved my little knife how could we make a fire? You fools go to the birch trees and get some touchwood," which they soon brought. A fire was made; we repaired our canoe, and carried all above the fall and the rapid; they carried the canoe; my share was the gun, axe, and pewter basin, and sextant box.

Late in the evening we made a fire and warmed ourselves. It was now [that] our destitute condition stared us in the face: a long journey through a barren country without provisions, or the means of obtaining any, almost naked, and suffering from the weather; all before us was very dark, but I had hopes that the Supreme Being through our great Redeemer to whom I made my short prayers morning and evening would find some way to preserve us....

We continued our voyage day after day, subsisting on berries, mostly the crowberry, which grows on the ground and is not nutritious, to the sixteenth of July. Both Paddy and myself were now like skeletons [from] the effects of hunger and dysentery, from cold nights, and so weak that we thought it useless to go any farther but [better to] die where we were. Kozdaw now burst into tears, upon which we told him that he was yet strong, as he had not suffered from disease. He replied, "If both of you die, I am sure to be killed, for everyone will believe that I have killed you both. The white men will revenge your death on me, and the Indians will do the same for him." I told him to get some thin white birch rind, and I would give him a writing, which he did; with charcoal I wrote a short account of our situation, which I gave him, upon which he said, "Now I am safe."

However, we got into the canoe, and proceeded slowly; we were very weak; when, thank God, in the afternoon we came to two tents of Chipewyans, who pitied our wretched condition. They gave us broth, but would allow us no meat until the next day. I procured some provisions, a flint and nine rounds of ammunition, and a pair of shoes for each of us on credit, to be paid for when they came to trade, also an old kettle. We now proceeded on our journey with thanks to God, and cheerful hearts.

From David Thompson's journals describing a 1796 trip from Black River to Lake Athabasca

ILLUSTRATION BY F. S. COBURN, 1896.

Summer Rambles

The voyageurs measure the distance by *pipes*.
At the end of a certain time there is a pause, and they light
their pipes and smoke for about five minutes, then the
paddles go off merrily again, at the rate of about fifty strokes
in a minute, and we absolutely seem to fly over the water.
"*Trois* pipes" are about twelve miles.

ANNA JAMESON,
WINTER STUDIES AND SUMMER RAMBLES IN CANADA, 1837

GORP AND THE "HIGH-GRADER"

Gorp (granola, raisins, peanuts), CPR (raisins, peanuts), scrog (anything goes) — whatever its name, it's the equivalent to the voyageur's pipe tobacco. Every hour the voyageurs would stop for a pipe rest. The average canoeist doesn't smoke now, but the ritual of stopping and diving into a bag for a handful of gorp is fun to look forward to. This pleasant interval provides a rest, a chance to refuel and time to look around.

The combinations of ingredients that can go into gorp are endless. There is the basic or inexpensive stuff made up of raisins and peanuts, and the more exotic and expensive, which might include such luxuries as candied pineapple, apricots, cashews, almonds, Smarties, coconut and banana chips. (In hot weather avoid the chocolate chips.) You can tell a great deal about a canoeist by the type of gorp he or she carries.

There is something you should know about gorp if you're paddling with others. You have to watch out for high-grading. High-grading is the despicable practice of removing only the exotic stuff when reaching for a handful of gorp. There are several ways to detect a high-grader. One way is to watch how long the hand stays in the bag. Another way is to use transparent plastic bags. Of course, the hard-core high-grader will take advantage of this to spot the good stuff and go straight for it, but most aren't that blatant. Watch their eyes. If they are clever at it, they glance at the bag, then turn away. What they are doing is memorizing the layout. I know people who can high-grade the candied pineapple out of a bag in one or two dips. The best way to control high-grading is to pretend you're being polite, grab the bag and give it a good shake as you hold it out. (But don't let go!) Then watch the pained expression as he or she comes up with just a handful of peanuts and raisins. I know canoeists who have tried to solve the whole high-grading problem by making their gorp with only choice items, but that's no fun at all.

Bill Mason, *Song of the Paddle*

CANOE-SWIMMING

Snake Island Lake

as we paddle out of the wilderness

and into

a land of

cars. and boats. planes. people. signs.

straight lines. human noise.

electric daylight at 10:30 pm.

ice cream. french fries. gasoline.

cottages. weekends. time from a watch.

telephones. news from home.

realizing how much we smell

like sweat and suntan lotion.

the earthen nomads

travel throughout time

and alongside it

observing the habits of the wind

and humans

and everything in between

TODD BARR,
WRITTEN ON DAY 28 OF A 50-DAY CANOE TRIP

Some time ago, six of us were loading gear from a floatplane into Royalex boats. We were soon on a river in the Precambrian Shield. In your best British accent: "The shield is a vast snowbound land of rock, tree, sky, and beast." However, in mid-May, the snow no longer binds the land, it fills the rivers — literally. This river was full of cold, clear water. Figuratively, it was full of piss and vinegar.

We started off, and for two days our group had a gay old time. The weather cooperated, *za menue* was extraordinaire, and there was never a shortage of campfire libation or clever repartee. The rapids? Ice beer is the simplest analogy — a beautiful clear amber, lots of foam, and just a few weeks removed from frozen solid.

Inevitably we approached a rapid that was different from anything upstream. We scouted the first section, which was very fast and very long. It began with a big ledge threaded by a narrow diagonal slot, flattened out for a stretch, then piled around a bend and down a chute.

We portaged gear around the ledge then went back above, intending to thread it in the canoe. The slot angled right to left, and we located it fine, then slid down. There was a large breaking wave at the bottom that wasn't visible from shore, and the way our boat was aimed we were going to hit it diagonally. It was the perfect moment for the bowman to dig in a cross-bow draw. Alas, this did not happen.

Immersed in 45-degree F water, how long do you have? When I was growing up, conventional wisdom had the human body ceasing all function within seconds. While my partner chose discretion and wisely struck out for shore, when I surfaced after the upset my first thought was to salvage the canoe. For sure it would be in pieces if I let it wash down the rest of the rapid. Even if, miraculously, it was still intact at the bottom, then what? Unless the river widened out and slowed up, it was headed for the Atlantic.

Without kneepads, I'd adopted the not-recommended habit of kneeling on my lifejacket instead of wearing it. I grabbed the boat and began canoe-swimming for the left bank, but now the stern-line snaked toward me, first caressing, then entwining my legs. I went under to untangle them and when I came back up, the chute we had scouted earlier appeared on the river horizon. I put everything I had into frog kicks, but with the river at a dead run, progress toward shore was achingly slow. Then another expression of affection from the stern-line.

The trick of running whitewater is not to try to rid your stomach of butterflies, but to make them fly in formation.

Anonymous

On re-surfacing I took inventory. My leg strength was dwindling and I was starting to really feel the cold. I was still twenty feet from the bank and now on an outside bend where the full force of the river poured into the chute, itself less than 100 feet away. It finally dawned on me that this is how people drowned. To this point the swim had been more frustration than anything else, but suddenly I was frightened, then very lonely. In twisted sympathy, the stern-line found my ankles, embraced them tightly, and I was towed feet first down the chute.

Finally the tumbling stopped. And now here I was, fifteen feet under, at the bottom of the pool below the chute. The stern-line had liberated me and the turbulence had freed my sneakers. The water, apart from traces of aeration, was crystal clear. Through occasional bursts of bubbles I could see the canoe and the trailing line on the river ceiling above me. The sky beyond the surface was bright blue, and some of the red pines that bordered the chute shimmered against it.

I was desperate for altitude, lungs bursting from a body that barely functioned. My limbs were anaesthetized, almost useless.

I felt suspended between the bottom of the pool and the top. The surface was close and beautifully unrippled, but it was also a torment, the looking glass I had to reach, then pass through to breathe. Breathing at that moment represented the sum of my needs and desires. I finally broke the surface and gulped air. Just downstream wallowed the canoe, on the brink of being sucked from the short pool of calm we shared into the next section of whitewater. To my left a rock slab rose from the pool, perhaps twenty feet away. Suddenly I felt it in my hands and I emerged from the water like some creature from the Devonian Age.

Below the second section of rapids we found a lake, and in the lake we found the boat. Apart from a few scratches, it was completely intact, triggering my acquisition of a Royalex canoe shortly afterwards. A throw-bag suddenly seemed important. I located knee pads which freed up the lifejacket. When I put it on I noticed a loop within easy reach. Someone showed me that it was a place to attach a sheath knife. Not a bad item to keep handy when canoe-swimming.

Richard Deacon

WILDWATER TECHNOJUNKIES, BEWARE

When I began running rapids, wood and canvas canoes were the norm. We knew that our boats were delicate, so swimming, or even crunching, simply was not an option. Did this restrict us? Not at all. My old Chestnut has happily danced through the Petawawa's flooded rollway and surfed the hole at the bottom of the Ottawa's McCoy's. It is three times my age, and almost as heavy, but still going strong. Folks quite often ask me if I'm worried about breaking my boat, and yes, I am, but I'm far more concerned about breaking my body. If I keep my boat out of trouble, I keep myself out of trouble.

Plastic boats and kayaks, helmets, drysuits and wetsuits, impact-resistant PFDs, knives, throw ropes, whistles: individually, they will make it possible for you to either run more challenging wildwater or to be rescued when you mess up, so they are extremely important; collectively, they might give you a false sense of security. Remember, your body is now the weakest link in the chain.

It used to be that you could not simply purchase a boat, immediately put in to serious wildwater, and hope to return home with more than a bundle of kindling tied together with strips of #10 cotton. It took a few years of experience before you would venture beyond Class III. Times

The human body is 70-percent water. Mike Elrich fine tunes for another stretch of chaos.

have changed. My novice kayak students run Class III on their first full day-trip, and Class IV by the end of their first season. The technique is easy enough to learn, and the equipment is superb, but I wonder: Do these new paddlers truly understand the forces with which they are playing? I doubt it.

They do not realize how quickly a run can go sour. The horror of dragging or pinning are only abstract constructs. The insidious nature of hypothermia is just something from a book. As an instructor, the hardest part of my job isn't teaching technique, it's conveying the absolute necessity of conservative judgment and teamwork.

When you go out this spring, please keep safety at the front of your mind. Think through the possible ramifications of your actions, and communicate and work closely with others on your paddling team. You will live or die by your decisions, so don't be led down the rock garden path by the durability of your equipment. Remember, a plastic-coated canoe has run Niagara Falls successfully; it's just the paddler who didn't survive.

Richard Culpeper, *Nastawgan*

There is both a sense of timelessness and tranquillity that goes with canoeing. These feelings come from fitting in with history, tapping a connection to our beginnings in the here-and-now and having a concern to preserve the future integrity of this activity. So, past, present and future meet...

BOB HENDERSON, "REFLECTIONS OF A BANNOCK BAKER," CANEXUS

CHICKEN SOUP FOR THE SOLE

Beyond Basswood and Wheelbarrow Falls, we stopped to share experiences with a group of canoeists at the end of the Lower Basswood portage trail. Holding the canoe away from shore, I stood knee-deep in the cedar-stained river. The muddy bottom and cool water felt good on my hot, blistered feet. Moments after paddling away from shore, I glanced down at my boots. Through the transparency of my wet nylon pants, I glimpsed hundreds of tiny wriggling black things. Trying to keep calm, I began slipping off the pants. Then a fat, black tail oozed down between my boot tongue and laces. Choking back a scream, I removed my boot ever so slowly, wincing with horror. Nothing! The blood-sucker was only on the boot. Sighing with relief, I casually pulled off the other one. Every moose, loon and human within a mile of our canoe must have heard the blood-curdling shriek. Squeezing my eyes shut, I flung my foot out to the side of the canoe for Gary to see. I couldn't speak. My foot was black with two-inch-long wiggling leeches. They squirmed between my toes while thick clumps of tiny ones clung to the blisters like petals on a chrysanthemum. I couldn't feel a thing, but the ghastly sight was soon made worse when I swiped my boot across them. I had forgotten that leeches cling to skin with a suction-cup mouth; my foot was now streaked with blood. Gary angled the canoe in toward shore and landed.

Andrea, Gillian, Lisa, and Lara running low on muck luck.

"We don't have any salt, do we?" Gary asked, hauling out the food pack.

"No! Just do something!"

"I know, soup mix!" Gary exclaimed, rifling through the pack's contents.

"Soup mix?!"

"Tomato or chicken?" Gary asked, holding up two different packages.

"I don't care!" I shrieked. "Just get them off me!"

Gary sprinkled the powdered soup liberally over my foot. The salty mixture worked like magic. The leeches curled up into little balls and dropped onto the rock in a seething pile.

"I don't suppose you'd like soup for lunch?" he asked wickedly.

Joanie McGuffin, *Where Rivers Run*

Paddle Your Own Canoe

I've travelled about a bit in my time.
And of troubles I've seen a few,
But found it better in ev'ry clime
To paddle my own canoe:
My wants are small I care not at all,
If my debts are paied when due,
I drive away strife, in the ocean of life
While I paddle my own canoe.

If a hurricane rise in the mid'day sky
And the sun is lost to view
Move steadily by, with a steadfast eye
And paddle your own canoe.
Fields of daisies that grew in bright green
Are blooming so sweet for you
So never sit down, with a tear or a frown
But paddle your own canoe.

IRISH BALLAD, CIRCA 1840
PUBLISHED IN JANE BENEDICKSON'S
IDLENESS, WATER AND A CANOE

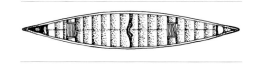

ALL I WANT IS A DRY BED

Nowhere is Life
So Dictated by the Elements

Canoeing the Barren Lands tends to be filled with such special moments — some pleasant, some profoundly unpleasant. Sitting in the tent, the walls straining in like a topgallant on a square-rigger running before the wind, a storm howling, pellets of icy rain beating relentlessly against the taut nylon shield between me and the outside, I endure the discomfort by forcing myself to remember the pleasures of the Barrens. Betting that the moorings of my shelter will hold, I muse thankfully on the extra five minutes I devoted to anchoring the tent before the storm began. It will end, in time, perhaps as suddenly as it arose. That is the nature of the Barren Lands: changeable, unpredictable, untamed, utterly wild.

One day all eight of us huddled together under a pair of upturned canoes as hailstones pelted our refuge. A few days later we ran barefoot on a trackless beach in heat that made even the frigid arctic waters tempting.

It is a world into which one must not venture without adequate preparation — not just the physical readiness needed for every canoe trip. This wilderness demands a certain attitude, an awareness that nature is going to be supreme. One must bend to its whims; one must approach the Barrens as a visitor, not a conqueror. Indeed, travel on the Barrens, summer or winter, is a humbling experience, as one realizes one's impotence before nature. Nowhere, in my experience, is life so dictated by the elements.

David Pelly, *Expedition*

Seven hundred thousand more make a mattress.

In 1977, Pelly's party retraced George Back's route of 1833–34 in search of John Ross's missing expedition.

Lecko gets busy after one too many rest days.

Along Québec's North Shore

By mid-afternoon, we eagerly waited for the tide to turn and the wind to subside. The river was rising on schedule, but the wind howled just as fiercely as ever. We decided to grit our teeth and do battle with the gale. By the time we had lugged the packs and canoe over the length of two football fields of mudflats to meet the incoming tide, we were an extremely bedraggled pair.

For an hour we fought the wind. Our muscles screamed for rest, but we pushed on. I dared not turn my eyes to shore for fear I'd give up. But our pathetically slow progress was hardly worth the effort.

"We're just wasting our time!" Gary yelled dejectedly. Abandoning the battle, we swung the canoe toward shore. We struggled up the beach where we huddled, cold and wet, and once again waited for the wind to subside. It didn't, but we pretended it had.

"Let's try and make a break for it!" Gary yelled with renewed anger. Cursing the waves, the gale and everything else, we staggered back out, yanking the canoe over the slippery mud as we went. The breaking surf pounded along the hull, threatening to capsize the canoe even before we had it launched. Just as we had pushed ourselves from shore, a sudden gust of wind lifted the waterproof map case off the thwart in front of Gary and threw it overboard. Fuming, he grabbed the case, laying it back in the canoe. Seconds later the same thing recurred, only this time the case flew straight in his face with a resounding slap. Cursing loudly, Gary grabbed the plastic case, threw it on the bottom of the canoe, then stomped on it with a muddy boot. "Who needs a bloody map on a day like this when I can see where we started and where we'll end!"

Gary and Joanie McGuffin, *Where Rivers Run*

The season
that precedes
and follows
mosquito season.

63

As Wet as Water Could Make Them

The tide of last night did not rise Sufficiently high to come into our camp, but the Canoes which was exposed to the mercy of the waves &c. Which accompanied the returning tide, they all filled, and with great attention we Saved them untill the tide left them dry. Wind hard from the South, and rained hard all the fore part of the day, at 2 o'clock P.M. the flood tide came in accompanied with emence waves and heavy winds, floated the trees and Drift which was on the point on which we Camped and tossed them about in such a manner as to endanger the canoes verry much, with every exertion and the Strictest attention by every individual of the party was scercely sufficient to Save our Canoes from being crushed by those monsterous trees maney of them nearly 200 feet long and from 4 to 7 feet through. Our camp entirely under water dureing the hight of the tide, every man as wet as water could make them all the last night and to day all day as the rain continued all day, at 4 o'clock P.M. the wind Shifted about to the S.W. and blew with great violence imediately from the Ocean for about two hours, notwithstanding the disagreeable Situation of our party all wet and cold (and one which they have experienced for Several days past) they are chearfull and anxious to See further into the Ocian, The Water of the river being too Salt to use we are obliged to make use of rain water. Some of the party not accustomed to Salt water has made to free a use of it on them it acts as a pergitive.

At this dismal point we must Spend another night as the wind & waves are too high to proceed.

Meriwether Lewis, *The Journals of Lewis and Clark*,
November 9, 1805, at the mouth of the Columbia River

Our Tent

May this tent be true to its idea
of sweet slumber, nurturing nights
cocoon with nylon cover,
its lovers might.

May this tent be fruitful,
and accepting of seed.
be firm to the union
its occupants heed.

May this tent be excellent and fair,
of the life long love
its poles shall bear.

STEPHEN D. DARRAUGH

I guess two requirements for northern adventure
are a strong back and a weak memory.
SALLY AND IAN WILSON, *ARCTIC ADVENTURES*

Vestibule model with nylon taffeta fly, add $3.

Rush hour on a high-pressure morning up north. The 3:30 sunrise arrives as we creep closer to camp.

WITH NO RHYME OR REASON

With stomachs full of coffee, we left the campsite at sunrise. The smooth water echoed upside-down images and the air was heavy and hot when you breathed in. After a morning of paddling through compressed heat, we finally felt the air loosen up and breeze around our near-naked bodies. We rested in canoes far from shore. The coloured canoe reflections began to swirl and mutate into pastel Van Goghs. The lake no longer seemed relaxed. The wind made it nervous and the surface rippled as it shivered. A sudden gust of wind, accompanied with a blast of cool air, banged the canoes together and then separated them just as quickly. We slipped into some clothing and noticed miniature twisters running along the surface of the murky water. Was there a weather rhyme that I had forgotten?

The weather was deteriorating very fast. The rumbling in the distance sounded like a bear spirit's stomach at the tail-end of a long and cold winter sleep. On the horizon, behind us, the tongues of jagged lightning lit up the underside of bruised clouds as they raced each other downward to lick the earth. Mother Nature was aroused and quickly building to an intense climax. Such a strange feeling — sitting in canoes, so far from shore.

With city arms weak from the life-or-death paddling stroke, we were still two hundred yards away from a small island when the storm wrapped around us. The lake was black and rolling. The canoes plunged down steep troughs and then accelerated upward for another breath. Each canoe went missing until it reached the top of a foaming crest and then disappeared again. Three canoes

> Bubbles rising in your coffee cup
>
> In fair weather you will sup
>
> But if they break and burst apart
>
> Rainy weather soon will start

powered by six paddlers with shoulders hunched to protect their ears from the thunderclaps. About three inches of water washed around the inside of each canoe creating a primitive roasting pan for that jolt of electricity to poach its quarry.

When the last canoe reached the protected shore of the rocky island it was raining sideways. We unpacked the boats wildly. Everything was chucked into the forest and out of the wind. We dragged the canoes farther up onto shore but left the water inside so that they wouldn't blow away. Wet, cold, and scared we huddled together on a small anchorage that was roofed in old growth pines. Big, beautiful, and very tall trees. Common sense told us this was the wrong place to be but it was either here on solid ground or the water. Peeking upward from inside drowned raincoats, and pulled down hats, we saw that most of the old veterans had lost their heads from past wars fought. Minute by minute everything became more violent. We could feel our place in the great scheme of things diminish. Mother was full-out pissed off. A fork of lightning momentarily blazed our vision as it hit and splintered one of the seasoned soldiers behind us. We could smell electricity. We heard the clunking and crying of rolled aluminum canoes on rock. We saw Michipeshu tumbling across the lake. An inner voice told me to push one of the other paddlers out into the open as a sacrifice. As I looked at possible victims I could see in their eyes that they too had heard the same voice. We all embraced each other tighter and waited. Each of us waiting.

Our muddled prayers must have helped. The spirits were compassionate and the worst of the storm was now in some distant place of torment. Feeling a little bit like Dorothy in *The Wizard of Oz*, we left the forest not knowing what we would find. There was no sign of Toto or our canoes, nor thankfully, a pair of shrivelling striped socks under the old pine that was uprooted, laying still, with its contorted branches snapped and twisted. The majestic carcass ungraceful, somewhat like a beached whale, marooned on the hard granite and lichen.

Such a strange feeling — sitting on an overturned island with the possibility of our canoes, once again, far from shore. How did we get fooled out there in the open water? The weather had appeared to be beautiful until five minutes before the storm. There was no warning other than the sudden fireballs from the East. No rhymes or indications that made sense. "Trout jump high when a rain is nigh." There were no trout. "When the peacock loudly bawls, soon we'll have both rain and squalls." No peacocks. "Cats and dogs eat grass before a rain." Maybe raining cats and dogs, but there were no cats or dogs gagging up grass previously. Not even a dead spider. Instead the signs seemed obvious: "No weather is ill if the wind is still." And the rhyme that we all live by: "The weather will be clear when there is enough blue in the northwest to make a Scotsman a jacket." Hell, there was adequate stock for hundreds of suits up there. But we did find truth in one of the old sayings: "Rain long foretold — long last. Short notice — soon past."

We walked around the island hunting for missing equipment. A couple of paddles wedged under a log. A faded orange life-jacket

Bailed out by silent partner after hydrokinetic takeover bid in the private sector.

skewered by branches of a fallen comrade. Several shredded pieces of the topo soaking in a flooded puddle. A baseball hat turned inside-out. An old bleached jaw bone of a moose. Bear scat. Three canoes! They had been launched into the underbrush and showed indications of collision with several large boulders at the end of the island. Scraped, creased and dimpled, but no serious injury to any of them. We had lost bits and pieces of loose clothing and a favorite pair of runners, but had recovered all the other equipment. A broken fishing rod and a split tube of toothpaste were the only casualties. There wasn't any sign of a campsite on the island nor did we want to stay any longer and risk the merriment of another storm, but there was the reality of having to stay and wait until the paddling conditions became safer.

The skies were clearing and the great Oz had given us a ribbon of new-found courage. We loaded the canoes and pushed off from our hiding place, paddling close to shore and talking steadily about what had happened within the last two hours. We mimicked owls with our heads as they turned in all directions looking for big weather. The skies were now blue without any trace of cloud. The wind had blown itself out. The water calm. We paddled for many more hours in near-naked bodies.

We arrived at the campsite by sunset. The smooth water echoed upside-down images and the air was heavy and crammed with mosquitoes when you breathed in.

Don Standfield

Adrift on his own personal flotation device.

Quinn psyches up for a dinner of rehydrated big-people food at the end of a grueling day.

Life's Simple Pleasures

Twenty miles downstream, chilled to the core, we pulled to shore, this time choosing a thickly wooded mainland site within which to find shelter. I desperately wanted a fire. After stringing the bedraggled tarp between trees to cover our packs, I explored the woods for reasonably dry kindling. After thirty-six hours of hard rain, dry twigs were rare indeed. Eventually, I came upon some large spruce, the kind of conifer that makes a roomy circular umbrella with its lower branches. Inside these minute havens, close against the tree trunks, I found small handfuls of dry dead twigs. Collecting several piles, I carefully put them in a plastic bag and placed the treasure inside my shirt. For larger kindling, I found dead standing trees, big around as my wrist, and sawed them down.

Under our meagre shelter, we cut up the wood and split the small sticks with our hatchet, exposing slivers of the dry core. When the rain slackened, I arranged my pile of prickly twigs, struck a match on the protected

underside of a rock, gingerly pushed the flame into the stack with trembling numb fingers. The little pile of spruce smoked and hissed with vehemence, took an agonizing time to send up tentative candle flickers, but finally took. We kneeled in front of the struggling fire, and coaxed it with little finger prods, fed in slivers of branch, gave encouraging breaths. It caught. Slowly we added bigger sticks.

One match after a thirty-six-hour rain! We chortled at each other with self-congratulatory glee, rubbed and clapped our cold, wrinkled hands together, and dove into the packs for hot drink supplies. We hadn't eaten properly for nearly two days. I had an almost insatiable appetite for hot food and drink. Two cups of coffee, one cup of cocoa, two Cup O' Soups, and three large helpings of gooey macaroni and cheese later, I was a restored man.

Alan Kesselheim, *Water and Sky.* Kesselheim's 2,000-mile trip through northern Canada, from Jasper to Baker Lake, started in June 1985 and finished in August 1986, with a winter stopover on Lake Athabasca.

Imagine the cold rain driving in your face, trickling down your neck. Feel your feet going numb in soggy neoprene boots and your stomach growling because you have paddled 40 miles and the last meal you ate was eight hours ago. Now imagine a nice dry tent, a warm sleeping bag, a pair of wool socks and a mug of hot chocolate. It's not too difficult to appreciate the simple things in life under such circumstances.

GARY AND JOANIE McGUFFIN,
WHERE RIVERS RUN

THE LABRADOR RIVER-RUNNER'S JIG

Carol and I invented a sort of dance that revived us a little — face your partner and jump up and down in a short-legged sort of way, energetically slapping your partner's clothing-padded shoulders. When you start giggling, you know you're on the road to recovery. And we did giggle. Two short bulky female forms, in ritual garb of modest neoprene undergarments covered with fourteen layers of outerwear, hopping around the soggy willow bank.

Jesse Ford, "What Did Flies Matter When You Were Free?", *Rivers Running Free*
Ford retraced Mina Hubbard's route down the George River during this trip of the late 1980s.

THE JOYS OF PORTAGING

The end of the human race will be that it will eventually die of civilization.

RALPH WALDO EMERSON

ABITIBI FUR BRIGADE

The pace is too exhausting; the canoes string out; but all the narrow blades slash away, for the portage is at hand. With dangerous speed the first canoe rushes abreast of the landing; and just as one expects disaster, the bowman gives the word. Instantly the crew, with their utmost strength, back water.

As the canoe comes to a standstill, the voyageurs roll their paddle-handles along the gunwales, twirling the dripping blades and enveloping the canoe in a veil of whirling spray. Then, jumping into the shallow water, they line up and quickly pass the packs ashore. The moment the cargo is transferred to the bank, the crew lift the great canoe off the water and turn it bottom up, while four of them place their heads beneath and rest the gunwales upon their capot-bepadded shoulders,.

As they carry it off, one is reminded of some immense antediluvian reptile crawling slowly over the portage trail. There is now much excitement. Other crews arrive, and are rapidly unloading. As the landing is over-crowded, the portaging begins. Each man ties the end of his tumpline about a pack, swings it upon his back, and bending forward, rests its broad loop against his forehead. Upon the first his companion places two more packs; then, stooping beneath the weight of 240 pounds, the packers at a jog-trot set off uphill and down; over rugged rocks and fallen timber; through fern-covered marsh and dense underbrush. Coming to an opening in the wood, on the bank of another lake, they quickly toss their burdens aside, and back again they run.

Nowhere can you see more willing workers. You hear no swearing or grumbling about the exceedingly hard task before them. On the contrary, every man vies with the rest as to which shall carry the greatest load and most swiftly across the portage. One crew races with another. Shirts and trousers reek with perspiration. The Indians puff and pant as they go by, and no wonder — the portage is three-quarters of a mile in length.

Arthur Heming, *Scribner's Magazine*, 1901

Canoemaker and guide Jim Spencer on tumplines:
"I think we should talk about the mysterious values
of this piece of leather and the subsequent development
of neck muscles that women find irresistible."

Rope tricks.
Downloading around heavy water on the Noire River.

GHOSTS OF PORTAGES PAST

The urge began the moment we pitched our tents near the rebuilt North West Company stockade on the north shore of Lake Superior. Gagnon's Island lay like a watchdog off the entrance to Grand Portage Bay. Hat Point with the gnarled old Witches Tree at its tip was waiting as always for the brigades to come by. In the blue distance was the shadowy outline of Isle Royale. It was the same as the day in 1731 when La Vérendrye and his voyageurs made the terrible nine-mile carry around the rapids of the Pigeon River toward the unknown country beyond for the first time. That night those men were with us and when the haze of our campfire drifted along the beach, it seemed to join with the smoke of long forgotten fires and lay like a wraith over the canoes, tepees, and tents along the shore.

Objects in the mirror
may be larger than they appear.

When we broke camp the following morning and toiled up the Grand Portage to the top of the first plateau, they moved beside us. When we stopped to rest and looked back at the blue sparkling expanse of Lake Superior, we saw it through their eyes. That day we struggled through bogs and muskegs with them, fought our way over hills and rocks and ledges, suffered from black flies and mosquitoes, made the same poses or rests after each half mile, and dreamed of the moment we would glimpse blue water, drop our loads, and take to the canoes once more.

Though there were no shouts of welcome at the landing, voyageurs were still with us. All along the trail Vérendrye blazed was a consciousness of them and of the land to which the Quetico–Superior was but the gateway. More and more our thoughts became involved with them, until by the time the trip was over at the far end of Rainy Lake, we knew that within a year or two we must follow them into the Northwest.

Sigurd Olson, *The Lonely Land*

No Compass, No Matches, No Protection from the Elements

We crossed the Eddy Lake portage and turned to paddle east to Knife Lake bay. When I reached the end of the bay, I suggested the women wait in the canoe while I hunted the blaze marks and found the trail to the next lake. I left my compass and map in the bottom of the canoe since I would be gone only a moment.

I found a path which could be the portage. It seemed familiar and yet a little different from the one I remembered. I went further and came to a large pond, which didn't look right either. Thinking the trail was further to my left, I searched in that direction. Then I turned to head back to the canoe. I found myself hopelessly lost in unfamiliar country, on an overcast day, without a compass.

Momentarily I was overcome with utter panic. I felt nauseated as thoughts whizzed through my mind. No compass, no matches, no protection from the elements. Gone for a week so no one would make a search for several days, plus the unpredictable reaction of two novice canoeists for whom I was responsible. It took all my will power to calm down.

I was in a stand of large jack pines whose limbs obligingly extended to the ground. I climbed to the top of one jack pine and thought I could see a hidden valley between two hills which could contain the waterway where I had left the canoe. I shouted from the top of the tree but there was no answer. A light spot momentarily appeared on the horizon. When I climbed down I blazed the tree on four sides with my knife and marked the initials N,S,E, and W.

I used this large jack pine as my anchor point and headed south, which I thought was the right direction. I broke twigs to mark my path,

constantly sighting back, first toward the tree and then down my straight line of broken branches. In about an hour I came back to the exact jack pine from which I had started. I had completed a large perfect circle.

Once more I climbed to the top of the jack pine and with two fingers whistled a shrill whistle. Way off in the distance I heard an answer. Then it was clear that I had become entangled in a series of small ridges. I started toward the whistle and after every two or three ridges I crossed, I climbed another jack pine and whistled. Each time the answer was closer. When I reached the canoe, I discovered the women had not stirred. They sat all those hours visiting. My relief was unbounded.

We paddled out of this bay, went around a point and into the next bay to the north, where I found the portage easily. It was over a year before I would step any distance into the woods without a compass.

Justine Kerfoot, *Woman of the Boundary Waters*
Kerfoot ran and guided from Gunflint Lodge, Minnesota.

There are billions of things I hate about canoe tripping. All of them are bugs.

ANONYMOUS

But Is It Good for the Complexion?

Even after reconnoitering, I managed to take a wrong fork on the second trip, traipsing off, under the canoe, along a caribou path. A hundred yards later I realized my error, but was too stubborn to go back the way I'd come. I'll just angle across this opening to the right, I thought. Pick up the trail farther along.

Two steps into the clearing, I sank to my crotch in muskeg. One second I was hot-footing across some wet ground, the next I looked like a dwarf wearing a seventeen-foot red hat. "Son of a bitch!" I muttered from under the boat. The cold muck held firmly to my lower half, and I stood on some indistinct surface that trembled underfoot, doing little to inspire me with confidence that I'd completed my descent. Unceremoniously, I wrenched the boat off my neck and slammed it down next to me in the ooze.

Now that I had committed myself to bushwhacking and could hardly get much wetter, I wallowed on across the quaking bog, using the canoe for balance and buoyancy, hauling the boat alongside as I half-swam, half-floundered through the fifty yards of waist-deep muskeg that separated me from the trail.

Looking up I saw Marypat, watching the spectacle, an expression of combined incredulity, horror, and barely suppressed mirth on her face as she took in my northern rendition of monster from the black lagoon.

"Jesus!" was all I could sputter, once I'd regained my full height on dry ground. A withering look at Marypat stopped the worst of her hysterical convulsions, but when I presented myself to the group at the end of the portage, looking like I'd lost a battle with a vat of chocolate fondue, even I had to admit the humor in the situation. The event was memorable enough to earn me the sobriquet Muskeg Mike.

Alan Kesselheim, *Water and Sky*
Crossing the height of land to the Dubawnt River, Nunavut Territory.

The word *chiropractic* was coined in 1898.

81

ILLUSTRATION BY F. S. COBURN, CIRCA 1900.

SIMON FRASER ON THE FRASER RIVER, JULY 10, 1808

Set out early. Kept the left side of the river accompanied by several Indians who shewed us the way. The road was inconceivably bad. We had to pass many difficult rocks, defiles and precipices, through which there was a kind of beaten path used by the natives, and made passable by means of scaffolds, bridges and ladders so peculiarly constructed, that it required no small degree of necessity, dexterity and courage in strangers to undertake a passage through such intricacies of apparent danger as we had to encounter on this occasion. For instance we had to ascend precipices by means of ladders composed of two long poles placed upright and parallel with sticks crossways tied with twigs. Upon the end of these others were placed, and so on for any height. Add to this that the ladders were often so slack that the smallest breeze put them in motion — swinging them against the rocks — while the steps were so narrow and irregular leading from scaffold to scaffold, that they could scarcely be traced by the feet without the greatest care and circumspection; but the most perilous was, when another rock projected over the one you were leaving. The Indians deserve our thanks for their able assistance through these alarming situations.

The descents were still worse. In theses places we were under the necessity of trusting all our things to the Indians, even our guns were handed from one to another. Yet they thought nothing of these difficulties, but went up and down these wild places with the same agility as sailors do on board of a ship.

Simon Fraser, *Letters and Journals 1806–1808*

ON THE CAMPSITE

Life at a northern Native village,
circa. 1905.

DAYBREAK

From the dying camp fires a thin column of smoke rises high above the trees, or spreads lakewards to join the damp misty veil which hides the quiet waters from view. Around the fires are silent forms like shrouded corpses stretched at full length on the bare rock or on spruce branches carefully arranged. These are the Indians, they have completely enveloped themselves in their blankets, and lie motionless on their backs. Beneath upturned canoes, or lying like the Indians, with their feet to the fire, the French voyageurs are found scattered about the camp; generally the servant attached to each tent stretches himself before the canvas door. No sound at this season of the year disturbs the silence of the early dawn if the night has been cold and calm. The dull music of a distant waterfall is sometimes heard, or its unceasing roar when camped close to it as on the Rattlesnake Portage, but these are exceptional cases, in general all nature seems sunk in perfect repose, and the silence is almost oppressive. As the dawn advances an Indian awakes, uncovers his face, sits on his haunches and looks around from beneath the folds of his blanket which he has drawn over his head.

After a few minutes have thus passed, not observing his companions show any signs of waking or disposition to rise, he utters a low "waugh"; slowly other forms unroll themselves, sit on their haunches and look around in silence. Three or four minutes are allowed to pass away when one of them rises and arranges the fire, adding fresh wood and blowing the embers into a flame. He calls a French voyageur by name, who leaps from his couch, and in a low voice utters "lève, lève." Two or three of his companions quickly rise, remain for a few minutes on their knees in prayer, and then shout lustily "lève, messieurs, lève." In another minute all is life, the motionless forms under the canoes, by the camp fires, under trees, or stretched before the tent doors, spring to their feet. The canvas is shaken and ten minutes given to dress, the tent pins are then unloosened and the half dressed laggard rushes into the open air to escape the damp folds of the tent now threatening to envelope him. Meanwhile the canoes are launched and the baggage stowed away. The voyageurs and travellers take their seats, a hasty look is thrown around to see that no stray frying pan or hatchet is left behind, and the start is made.

Henry Hind, a geologist,
accompanied the Red River expedition of 1857.

MOOSE DROPPINGS

As the world careens toward online sponge baths, weight-loss pizza and all unfathomable manner of genetic tweakery, I cling to this rock like lichen, its granular pink plutonic granite crumbling nonetheless away under my chewed fingernails. My insurance firm is Feldspar & Quartz. Our planet spins in space at 660 miles per hour, brothers and sisters: who can grip tightly enough? But out here, life's details spin away just beyond grasp, too. Out here, I can place my bony 42-year-old hindquarters on the exposed 240-million-year-old basement rock of the original super-continent, sip 16-year-old Islay single-malt from a Happy Convenience mug, flip off the white noise and tune in to the nocturnal slapstick. There's no panacea like sitting on Pangea with the things that go bump and grind in the night. My ex-wife's name is Melia — a molecular geneticist, a cloner — but enough about her out here. Enough about my red-lined Visas and the whole wobbly unsecured line of credit that was tamped down the well hole last spring. No exes and owes out here. Out here, the mind is unleashed. Click. Out here, I stalk the fishes of the lake, knowing we once were them. Out here, rehydrated mystery meat and lentils taste like medallions of range-fed goose in Madeira-and-pear sauce. Out here, I suddenly believe that we could all be thankful; we have that option. And the talk turns to humbling personal truths and sage wisdom — like the time a friend's massive father had to be paddled and portaged out and was subsequently hospitalized after having employed, whistling merrily, a handful of foliage, largely poison ivy, as toilet paper. Out here, the truly odd seems worthily curious and the possible seems possible again. Black bears have been into the new moose calves this season, and the park's wildlife ecology thinkers have decided to retool their dining habits with smorgasbords of airlifted roadkill moose. You see, out here, life can be a picnic. In a whiff of campsmoke whimsy a half-ton moose may just drop out of the sky and its pendulous velvet muzzle buff your cheek as it passes. You may find yourself at the teddy bears' picnic. It beats 18.784 percent interest and tips on how to force-blossom your annuals with a blowdryer.

Noel Hudson, rock hugger

Kayaking is a form of waterborne locomotion in which the paddler sits, bent at the waist with legs outstretched, and uses strokes from a single, double-ended paddle to drag his or her butt across the surface of the water in a not altogether wholesome fashion. But they are our cousins and we love them like family.

A miraculous and quick-witted escape was once made...when an Indian attempting to cross found his paddle breaking in his hands.
Flinging it aside he grasped a broom that happened to be in the canoe and made his was safely to shore.

P.G. DOWNES, *SLEEPING ISLAND*, 1943

THE DAILY ROUTINE

Another day in the fast lane,
as the stones stop by for coffee.

We carry no lights except flash lights for emergency. Everything must be done by daylight so we try to get up by the sun and generally we manage to go to bed shortly after sundown. Watches are on standard time.

Reaching a campsite, the Bourgeois and Elliott unpack the food, while I find rocks for the fireplace and wood. With the fire going the Bourgeois and Elliott set about cooking dinner. Tony sets up the tent for the Bourgeois and himself. Eric puts up his tent and builds the only sanitary convenience one has in the wilds, while Omond and I after cutting poplar tent poles, put up the three-man Baker tent. There is of course likely to be a difference of opinion on which is the most level site and which way the opening should face.

All during this the Bourgeois has been cooking and Omond has slipped away to mix rum with whatever fruit flavoring, spices or water he can find. Everything has taken about 90 minutes and all is ready to sit down on the rocks to cocktails, dinner and sunset.

During spare moments Eric may have written up the log, noted the portage routes, and studied our history books to tell us bout the present area's past, Omond will have discussed the next day's navigation with the Bourgeois, I will have written the diary. Everything is done quickly. After 25-35 miles paddling and portaging it is after 6 p.m. before a campsite is found, 7:30 when dinner is ready, 8:00 eaten, 8:30 cleaned up and 9 P.M. bed.

Breakfast, washing up, stowing the packs and getting into the canoes takes two hours. For breakfast it is a heavy meal, porridge or corn meal, bacon, bread, and eggs when we have just left a provisioning stop, otherwise fish, marmalade and coffee.

Lunch is cold and takes an hour from landing to setting off. Cheese, reconstituted fruit drink, sausage, cold bacon, jam, dry biscuit or rye vita and a 30-minute rest. Daily schedule of the party depended much on the weather, the distance we had covered the day before and the distance we expected to do.

We went to bed at or slightly before sunset in sleeping bags on air mattresses and were ready to get up at any time around sunrise. Only twice did we do so at 4:30. Generally it was half past five.

All decisions were made by the Bourgeois, the leader of the party, a term used by the Voyageurs for the trader they served and paddled.

Our Bourgeois, Sig Olson was different in that he provided, besides direction, cooking, superb paddling, especially in rapids, and an unsurpassed knowledge of how to live comfortably and eat well on your own resources.

Until I saw Chardin's painting, I never realized how much beauty lay around me...in the half-cleared table, in the corner of a tablecloth left awry, in the knife beside the empty oyster shell.

MARCEL PROUST

Denis Coolican, *Canoe Trip Diary*, Thursday, August 4, 1955. On this trip were Eric Morse, Elliot Rodger, Coolican, Tony Lovink, Omond Solandt, and Sigurd Olson. Olson's *The Lonely Land* also chronicles the trip, and Eric Morse's *Freshwater Saga* describes this and other "Voyageurs" trips.

A Comfortable Bed

T alk about your soft, spicy beds of balsam boughs! I slept on bare slats, and I know how many, for I counted them at least a hundred times. Then there was a root under my fifth rib when I lay down, which at first seemed only a trifle, but that root grew in half an hour to the size of a log. If I turned over on my other side, the ground under my hip was higher than that under my ribs, and I was soon ready to collapse. Then I tried lying on my back, but an industrious spider was soon busy connecting my nose with the ridgepole of the tent. After a while I managed to get both eyes shut, and was sinking into a doze when — mother of Moses! — I thought a wild-cat was scaling the tent on the outside. What a fearful noise! Then another wild-cat ran up after the first, and the first went down the opposite side. I kicked you, but you wouldn't wake — you and the guides were too busy snoring. Heavens! I would rather take my chances camping on Boston Common without a tent. When I finally did go to sleep, it seemed but a few moments before my feet and right shoulder were freezing cold, and I found them uncovered. From that time until after daylight my constant prayer was that the guides might soon get up and build the fire. Where, I should like to know, are all the comforts and enjoyments held out so alluringly before me when you inveigled me from home? I can rough it well enough in the daytime, but when it comes to the night, I must say, I'm a little particular, and I don't want my bed on the side of a hill or on a woodpile. By the way, Joe, what were those creatures that made such a racket on the tent? Weasels?

"They must be — mice I think," replied Joe, "little fellows with these little short tails. They're lookin' for somethin' to eat."

Lucius Hubbard, *Woods and Lakes of Maine*, 1884

A hard night's day. Waking up to salt air and sunrise on the Atlantic coast.

Former Quebec Anglers' Association chairman Philip Bruneau
with fellow trippers Bill White and Sterling Pollock, circa 1950.

BUGLESSNESS

No northern trip had ever begun as bug-free as this. We paddled shirtless, sometimes in shorts, only rarely broke out one of the repellent bottles. I am used to seeing the northern world through the green haze of netting, to synchronizing bites of food with quick lifts of the headnet, to feeling the plastic of my writing pen melt under the caress of my DEET-coated fingers.

Alan Kesselheim, *Water and Sky*

PRECIOUS BATTER

I moved busily around the fire, barefooted, warm and dry in the hot sunshine and the wind. The Cache Rapid lay below us: we had arrived, and I would make Logging Cake à la Faille to celebrate: one would have to be careful of the batter, for fierce gusts were driving small whirls and eddies of ash out of the fire on the leeward side....

Suddenly a piercing yell shattered the peace of the summer afternoon. Gordon sat up: the hat fell off his face and he blinked wildly at the sun. A gust of wind had whirled a piece of glowing charcoal out of the fire and lodged it neatly between my toes: swearing with pain I gallantly set down the panful of precious batter and the ladle that I held in my other hand: a lesser man would have flung them down, in the grub box, on Gordon, anywhere...Thank God the river was near, and I rushed into its cooling waters with a hiss.

R.M. Patterson, *Dangerous River*. Patterson, an Englishman, based this book on his backcountry adventures on the South Nahanni River from 1927–29. He later settled on a ranch in the foothills of the Canadian Rockies.

THE PERFECT CAMPSITE

In country like this, one should be grateful for any patch of open ground level enough to lie down on. And yet it's always tempting to look for a nicer beach or view, or a place better supplied with fresh water or wood. If you are too choosy, you go on. And on and on, passing up perfectly adequate spots, until you run out of light and end by hacking a miserable camp out of the bush. Often as not when you set out in the morning, you pass the beach of your dreams just around the next point.

Michael Poole, *Ragged Islands*

THE TEA POT

At noon we boiled tea near a little spring of clear, cold water.

As yet we had no opportunity of seeing farther

than the closing in of many trees.

We were, as far as external appearances went, no more advanced

than our first resting-place after surmounting the ridge.

This effect is constant in the great forests.

You are in a treadmill – though a pleasant one withal.

Your camp of to-day differs only

in non-essentials from that of yesterday,

and your camp to-morrow will

probably be almost exactly like today's.

STEWART EDWARD WHITE, *THE FOREST*

We boiled tea. It is an insignificant comment (perhaps) within a description of the mood of a long portage or hike of a hard working trip. It seems an insignificant act. Canadian northern travel literature is full of the mention "we boiled tea," full of such "insignificants." The mood of our travel literature is also rich with reference to arduous travel and the eerie reverence for the shrouding effect of the forest and endless waterways. The simple act of boiling the tea pot (or tea pail as it is often called in early writings) may appear incongruous added to such descriptions of work, struggle and presence of an aura of nature. It is not!

"We boiled tea" may have a common ring to it but it can equally conjure up a rich set of understandings for Canadian canoe trippers. It means, let's rest, let's celebrate the moment, let's absorb this place — this aura, let's absorb our time together. It means a respite from the wind or trail and the acknowledgement of the accomplishment of the moment. The accomplishment may

"The Cook," circa 1905. It is said that a watched pot never boils, but it seems this did not hold true for the early traveler's "tea pail."

be the standard deep satisfaction of physical challenge or the still deeper satisfaction of being precisely where you are — feeling the swell of absorbing the place, that moment in time ... with tea, with a quiet sit down, alone or with travel companions, not talking much or maybe sharing a story or two, being aware of the restorative quality of stillness down by the water or in the woods embracing the ritual of the Canadian tripper's pot of tea.

My tea pot sits quietly in my wanigan in storage waiting for the next trip. It is an unassuming little thing, but I don't go to the bush without it. For it has come to represent for me a tangible expression of that enduring ritual, that restorative quality, which is manifested in a web of memories of places and people all gathered around a tea pot. You might hear a tripper say, "Sure, we'll use your canoe, packs, etc., but can I bring my tea pot?" The associations go deep, deeper even than one's own collections of experience.

The quiet repose around the evening campfire or trail fire centered around the activity of the tea pot is part of the larger-than-life tradition of all past travellers on northern waterways. When you stop for tea or celebrate an end of day with a soothing warm mug up, you are part of all this tradition. As Sigurd Olson once said about the canoe, you become part of all it knows: so too for the tea pot abrewed over the campfire. The web of associations is enlarged to a yet far greater enterprise. The swell of conciousness is real and you know tomorrow's headwind can be cursed or celebrated from "within" an enduring membership. The membership is a swell of strength, a physical and spiritual strength. And, that tough portage is walked with this strength giving you feeling under your skin so that the travels are more a pilgrimage than a trial, more a mystery than a conquest, more a rendering of the past than a single moment of the present, and you are more alive in the process. Yes, all of this from that tea pot.

The tea pot is that rallying point around which there is reflection and the stillness of ritual to bring forth into being all the associations of warmth, essentials and illuminations of your community and the presence of the named and unnamed historic precursors who have paddled by this way or in this way.

Norwegian philosopher Peter Wessel Zapffe has said, "Most people manage to save themselves by artificially paring down their consciousness." When I stop to think of our western culture's detached, though yearning, relationship with the earth — our abuses, our excessive want, our burning desire for control — I see the truth in this statement. When I take a moment to think of my associations with that beat-up little blackened tea pot stored away at present in an equally well-aged wanigan, I smile with a full weight of a particular consciousness that is less in need of paring down but rather should be celebrated. I think of the view over that swamp, the soft pine needles, the sense of earlier travellers watching over me, the group smiling over a fancy desert, a simple catching of a stare with a friend, the earth and our place within; all over the aura of a brew of tea with that tea pot. And when I'm thinking this way, I don't want to stop thinking.

Bob Henderson
educator, paddler, tea drinker

We are going to boil-up.
The sweet oriental scent of tea and the feel of bread
between my teeth sweeps over me like dizziness ...
the fire leaps at the base of a big spruce ...
we sink before it like worshippers

Elliott Merrick, *True North*, 1933

Raze and Shine

Our amusement was interrupted by an untoward accident, Mr. Franklin's tent having taken fire from some embers which had been placed in it, to expel the mosquitoes. Hepburn was asleep with several powder horns near his head, and did not awake, till the tent poles fell upon him, when he escaped without hurt. The tent, part of the flag, some cloaks and bedding were burnt....

Robert Hood, *To the Arctic By Canoe*

Campfires are sure to attract flying bush eels.

On Great Slave Lake

By the time I got through eating, I was attracted by our unusual fire. Instead of burning down, it seemed to be burning more intensely. The whole fire had sunk about a foot into the stone bank. That mystified us. Poking the fire with a long stick trying to figure out how the stones could be burning, we found that the shore was lined with one huge long pile of logs and driftwood, nearly ten feet deep. Over the top of the pile, a layer of gravel and stones had been pushed by the shifting lake ice at breakup time. In the darkness we had mistaken this for a solid stony shoreline and had built our fire about halfway up it.

We were alarmed to discover that a huge pile of driftwood was on fire beneath the layer of stones. Close to the driftwood, all along the shore was a heavy stand of mature spruce. We had the potential makings of a forest fire!

We both grabbed cooking pots and started running back and forth throwing water on the fire. After considerable running around I saw that we were losing the battle, so I grabbed a long stick with a hook on the end, and started raking away the stones and pulling out logs and pieces of wood and throwing them in the water. For a while it looked as though we had lost control, but after two hours of frantic fire fighting we finally had every last ember put out. In the struggle, soot and ashes had covered us from head to foot and we had dug a hole in that beach of stones and driftwood ten feet in diameter and three feet deep.

Clayton Klein and Verlen Kruger, *One Incredible Journey*

How to Start a One-Match Fire in a Driving Rain

We were camped one evening in the Boundary Waters area, west of Thunder Bay, and that typical ice-cold piercing rain was coming down in lightly blowing sheets — the kind of rain that every canoeist dreams about all winter long. We were camped under a couple of really nice rain flies and had a cheery fire going (the group painstakingly made shavings and split fine kindling from the centre of sawn logs, laying them carefully in a pyramid). We had hot chocolate on, and were having a great time watching it rain.

About 8 o'clock, two groups of canoeists came in — two men, one had a little girl about ten years old and the other had a boy about 11. The kids were really cold, near hypothermic. They were obviously very disappointed because they had planned to make this campsite and we were there. I said, "Come on, camp here. Your kids are cold, you're cold. We'll help you set up the tents." We got the kids warmed up and the one guy started working on the tent. I said to him, "We'll help you get a fire going. We've got lots of dry wood here and a fire going. We'll just peel you off some and get one started." He said, "No thanks, Cliff. It's O.K., I can take care of it."

I watched him out of the corner of my eye and I couldn't believe it. It was a combination of anger and jealousy. He had a little butane stove, see. So he took the top off this butane stove and he plugged it into a blowtorch head. He walked over and grabbed an armful of the wood we had offered him and just threw it in a pile. Then he fired up this blowtorch, stuck it underneath this log, walked away and set up his tent. Fifteen minutes later, he had a cheery fire going. I didn't know whether to laugh or cry. Here we'd spent hours getting our fire going. He just turns on a blowtorch. Well, anyway, that's one way you can always get a fire going in the driving rain.

Cliff Jacobson, Canoeexpo

Secret Ingredients

A high note in the orchestral symphony of fine food preparation was hit during our Wolf River trip. A voracious population of mosquitoes greeted us at Fish Lake. We set up camp on the run. From the bottom of a pack we retrieved a pre-mixed homemade chocolate cake mix, smuggled in for Tracee's birthday celebration. The birthday girl and others not needed for supper preparation quickly retreated to the middle of the lake, where a pleasant breeze kept the bugs at bay.

Seasoned outdoor chefs efficiently channel the excess energy generated by the incessant buzzing of mosquitoes. With one fluid motion, I swatted and grabbed the vanilla. A vituoso performance.

After settling the cake into a carefully prepared bed of coals, I began putting the ingredients away. It was then I noticed the other vial of brown liquid. I realized with chagrin that Tracee's birthday surprise contained a generous portion of the wrong flavoring.

I avoided admitting my mistake until after the supper festivities were finished. I encouraged everyone to guess the secret ingredient that made the cake so darned delicious. We had conjectures ranging from apricot baby food to Grand Marnier.

No one came up with the correct answer — soy sauce.

Ken Madsen, *Rivers of the Yukon*

Wanted: Viking helmet, size XXL. Dave Taylor takes a moment to model the latest in northern "found" fashion before rejoining fellow trippers.

Voyageurs' Fine Eats

This galette is the only form of bread used on a voyage, that is when voyageurs are so fortunate as to have any flour at all. It is made in a very simple style — the flour bag is opened, and a small hollow made in the flour, into which a little water is poured, and the dough is thus mixed in the bag; nothing is added, except perhaps some dirt from the cook's *unwashed* hands with which he kneads it into flat cakes, which are baked before the fire in a frying pan, or cooked in grease. To pampered dyspeptics a breakfast of galette and salt pork might not seem very inviting; but let them try it on a northern voyage, after traveling five hours in the morning without eating, and they will find it otherwise. There is no denying that voyageurs are not apt to be very cleanly, either in their persons or in their cooking; but it is wonderful how any fastidiousness on the subject wears off when a traveler is voyaging in the wilderness.

Robert Kennicott, naturalist and explorer.
In 1859 the Smithsonian Institution sponsored Kennicott on his expedition to Fort Yukon to collect fauna and carry out his studies.

It's Lore Time

I am in the process of stirring up the coffee in a camp pot with my rusty axe file, which is the handiest implement I can get my hooks on. I am not aware that I am being watched by my client, the father, who asks pleasantly, "What are you doing?" What I am doing, of course, is getting caught out.

I say to myself, "It's lore time, folks." I say to the father, "This old axe file makes the best coffee...I would never be without it"...Lie, I lie more and am getting to like my lie. On and on I go, embellishing, elaborating, and sink myself deeper with each word, because for the next 26 times we have coffee, I'm supposed to produce that damned axe file, and do you think I can ever find it?

Jeff Miller, *Rambling Through Algonquin Park.*

BANNOCKS

At first I thought I could teach the men a lot of things about cooking bannocks, but it was not long before I began to suspect that I had something to learn. They were made simply with flour, salt, baking-powder and water, but without any shortening. This made them tough, but they carried better so. As George said: "You can throw them round, or sit on them, or jump on them, and they are just as good after you have done it as before."

Mina Hubbard, *A Woman's Way Through Unknown Labrador,* 1905.
Mina Hubbard's husband died of starvation while attempting an ascent of the Naskapi River, Labrador, in 1904. Mrs. Hubbard, accompanied by her husband's guide, successfully completed the 550-mile route up the Naskapi and down the George River the following summer.

WINDHAM THOMAS WYNDHAM-QUIN, 4TH EARL OF DUNRAVEN

Landing in the evening, you struggle back from the romance of leaf tints and sunset glows to the delicious savouriness of a stew composed of fat pork, partridges, potatoes, onions, fish, and lumps of dough; and having ballasted yourself with this compound, and smoked the digestive pipe, sleep on sweet pine-tops till you're levéed by the steersman in the morning, when you pursue your way, not miserable and cross, as you might be at home after such a mess of pottage, but bright, happy, and cheerful; capable of enjoying to the full the glories of the daybreak....

The Great Divide, 1874

Sufficient ballast.

ILLUSTRATION BY F. S. COBURN, CIRCA 1900.

LONGEVITY

Charlie always used tea sticks for cooking. He would cut a length of stout green willow and with the ax cut one end into a point. He would harden the point in the fire then drive it into the ground at an angle with the blunt end of the ax and hang the billies on it by their bail handles. He would move the billies up and down the stick or regulate the fire in order to control his cooking. We would carry the stick with us until the green wood charred through....

Charlie's ideas about food differed from my own. He thought that while in the bush a man should have a high-carbohydrate, high-fat diet. He also believed in cooking things for a long time. When we had pike or rabbit he would cut it into sections and put it into a pot, then whenever we built a fire he would simmer the meat, sometimes for two days before eating it. I did not know whether these practices were good or not, but how can you argue nutrition with a 70-year-old man who can outpaddle you?

Thomas McGuire, *99 Days on the Yukon*

A Toast to...

Omond, whose first doctorate was in medicine, was naturally our medical officer, not that I ever remember anyone needing much in the way of medical attention. He also had the important position of brewmaster. The evening drink before dinner, all chores done, was a hallowed time, and the precious ration called for serious attention. In the first year of our canoeing together, Tony had introduced us to overproof rum, the nearest thing to dehydrated alcohol and obviously the answer for long canoe trips. It did not take us long to evolve what we considered the best rum cocktail: a daiquiri made by adding lemon powder, sugar, and water, which has now become well-known among Canadian canoeists as "voyageurs' punch." It has the delightful property of making one oblivious to the bugs, although there is one theory that the lemon actually drives the bugs away. Omond, however, always seemed to be experimenting with other mixtures, and we suffered rum with fruit drinks, with spices, with beef bouillon, and once disastrously with cocoa. He explained that these aberrations were only because the lemon powder had become almost unprocurable. Our ration of rum was two ounces per person, but we did carry a little extra for celebrations and emergencies. Omond once brilliantly declared a celebration because there was no emergency.

Eric Morse, *Freshwater Saga*

Pemmican

Pemmican can be made from beef or other red meat. The meat is sliced thin and cut into narrow strips — say an inch wide by eight inches long — and sun-dried ("jerked") for two or three days (a clothes line will do, but dry weather is a must). At that point it will keep and is not bad to eat. The next step is a day or two of smoking — the meat is hung on racks over a low fire, the heat and smoke kept in by a covering tarp (an oven at a low temperature would do). It is then crumbled, mixed with an equal quantity of rendered fat, and sealed in waterproof bags, in which form it should keep for up to a year; raisins or any dried berries obtainable can be mixed in to improve the flavour and nutrition (the Chippewas of northern Wisconsin and Minnesota used maple sugar). With or without the berries, pemmican is a complete food. For a person of average size, two and a half pounds per day is enough for the heavy work of canoeing.

Robert Mead, *Ultimate North*

MEATLESS PEMMICAN

My philosophy of trip food is predicated on the principle that you should go as light as possible, cook only when you can kill something, and on any decent trip you should be hungry enough to eat a skunk's asshole by the end of the day. This somewhat twisted attitude to wilderness cuisine is no doubt a result of travelling with the Inuit in my formative years. They ate only once a day, drank massive quantities of sweetened tea, and ate virtually everything we killed, raw. It's amazing how comforting seal's liver, steaming at blood heat, can be when wrapped around a chunk of blubber, while hunkered down beside a komotik. Of course, it also helps to be caught in a blizzard on the sea ice, lost, and if said liver belongs to the only seal you've killed in three days.

Although the power bars fall short of the aforementioned principle of "no cooking, kill as you go," it does provide a practical and politically correct alternative.

I like to tell our staff that guiding is ninety-five-percent cooking, five-percent terror.

NEIL HARTLING, NAHANNI

The recipe goes something like this:

Mix together in a bowl:

3 cups flour (whole wheat or all purpose or any combination thereof)

3/4 cup of wheat germ (or any kind of nut meat, such as sunflowers, etc., which has been run through a coffee grinder and turned into flour)

1 cup of skim milk powder

1 cup of full-fat soya flour (or more nut meat ground to flour, or more milk powder)

3 cups of finely chopped raisins, dates, dried apples, currants, apricots, (whatever you've got or any combination thereof)

Add to this:

6 large eggs

3/4 cup of vegetable oil (preferably olive oil)

2/3 cup of blackstrap molasses — not the more highly refined kind

The ingredients are now mixed together into an unbelievably sticky, hard-to-stir mess. The batter should be very stiff and will require a fair bit of upper body strength to beat into submission.

Once thoroughly mixed, turn out into a 10-by-15-inch well-greased cookie pan. The mixture should thoroughly cover the pan to a depth of about 3/4 of an inch. Because of the stiff, sticky nature of the batter, it helps to cover your hands in oil and pat the batter into the cookie sheet.

Finally, cook in the oven set at 225 degrees Fahrenheit for between 2 1/2 and 3 hours. In essence this really isn't cooking just drying out the batter. Cut bars into appropriate sizes after thoroughly cooled.

It has been my experience that this power bar keeps for a long time. I've never had it go moldy even when I have been out for a month. Something I've been wanting to try is to periodically brush a batch of bars with brandy much as one would do with a dark fruitcake. Indeed, this "meatless pemmican" bears a striking resemblance to dark fruitcake, which no doubt, considering the aging requirements for good dark Christmas cake, bodes well for its prospective qualities.

Chris Blythe

TREATING WATER

Consider the use of heat. Heat is a very good way of killing germs that want to live in your gut. As a matter of fact, if you raise the water temperature to 150 degrees Fahrenheit, you're going to kill anything that wants to live in your stomach. That does not make water sterile, but it sure makes it safe to drink. It's amazing to me how people keep adding time onto this: "You've got to boil water thirty minutes," and stuff like this. Actually, most of the cysts and so forth are killed at 140 degrees Fahrenheit. You bring water up to the boil [100 degrees Celsius or 212 degrees Fahrenheit], you've killed everything. That's all you've got to do. There are various filter systems and chemical systems that work if you use them properly, but the thing is...heat always works.

William Forgey, M.D.

CAMP COCKTAILS

The high winds had churned the lake [Winnipeg] into a brown silty soup garnished with bits of green algae, sticks and diluted gull guano. This fishy, smelly liquid was our only source for drinking water. Consequently, we had to go through a long and tedious process of water gathering. Armed with yards of toilet paper and a couple of T-shirts, we constructed a filtering system through which we poured this revolting mixture. After several filtrations, finely ground silt still hung suspended in the water so we took the brown liquid and proceeded to boil it thoroughly. We poured off the liquid, careful not to disturb the sediment settled on the bottom of the pot. Now came the final stage — four large sweet spoonfuls of purple grape-juice powder were poured into every bottle for drinking water to mask the colour and taste. The rest was left for cooking.

Gary and Joanie McGuffin, *Where Rivers Run*

CREATURES
GREAT AND SMALL

Man is the only animal that can be bored.

Alone in the woods
hidden in heavy shadows
afraid
and waiting for them to return
wondering if they made it
over the portage
while lost canoes
from a silouette shore
drift together through the dark

Standing back behind the pines
as the water moves the landscape
I look down the path
and shiver
wondering if they are safe
or have they too
been swallowed
by the blackness on some other lake

I want to slip into the water
and suffocate my imaginary fears
so that my cowardice
will not offend
the brother wolf
who prowls the forest
looking for fire
by the light of the stars

Bear - you are in my mind

and I can hear you
moving towards my hiding place
as I crouch deeper
wrapping my arms around my legs
and hunching shoulders
so that your grasp
will be unable to find
the back of my neck

I fear nothing that is real
but feel confident
that it will be terrifying
when the black silence shatters
and you lunge out
from behind the tree trunks
and hold me
firmly in your mouth

BEARS

We drifted past a grove of trees, savouring the smell of sun-warmed spruce needles and marvelling at this growth, hundreds of kilometres north of the tree line. Suddenly a grizzly bear burst from the willows along the shoreline. We stopped paddling and sat motionless, each holding our breath.

The bronze-coloured giant saw us, and for an instant it probably wondered what the strange yellow object floating on the river was. Then, without warning, the grizzly charged down the embankment straight toward us. We were only a few metres from the shore. That was uncomfortably close to a bear who to strides at two metres each.

Sally and I exchanged nervous glances. There was no need for words. Together, we dug our paddles into the river, thrashing furiously in the wat we struggled to widen the distance between us and the advancing bear.

The sight of our flashing paddles must have startled the bear. When I glanced over my shoulder to check our progress, the grizzly had halted and was studying us from the shore. The huge animal was standing on its rear legs and sniffing the air in loud snorts. Then the bear spun around and bolted up the hill

"Perhaps we need a bath. That bear took off pretty fast when it smelled us," Sally said with a grin.

The encounter with the grizzly was fresh in our minds when we stopped for the night. Sally and I took great care to look for signs of bear along the beach, and we set up camp only when we were both satisfied that the area was bear-free.

At four in the morning, a grunting noise startled us from our sleep. Our first thought was that the grizzly had found us and was helping itself to our food. We lay motionless for many long minutes hoping the sound would go away. It didn't.

Slowly, quietly, we unzipped the tent door and then peered out into the dull light of an overcast morning. The grunting continued.

"Can you see anything?" I whispered.

"No bears, but I can't figure out what the noise is."

A moment later Sally jabbed my side.

"What?" I whispered hoarsely.

"Caribou. Maybe forty of them among the rocks on the opposite shore."

Sally and Ian Wilson, *Arctic Adventures*

SEARCHING FOR SPECKLES

Are the fish rising to the surface or staying deep? Dry flies? Wet flies? A Green Despair, Royal Wulff, Humpy, Whooly Worm, or the cud-ball the cat coughed up last night? Flyfishing for trout is a complicated process and it takes years to turn lucky guesses and patience into a fine art. The cold rivers and gravel bars are home to fine specimens who effortlessly dangle between the river bottom and suffocating air, on the shadow side of boulders or beneath the cut banks and overhanging cedar trees. These creatures skulk the waters for minnows, leeches, crayfish, gnats, nymphs — anything that will fill their insides and not bite back. Still, there is no guarantee that all your previous experience — and even wearing good-luck underwear — will attract a breakfast.

To catch 'em you have to start thinking like a fish. You really have got to want that Stone Fly in your chops. You have to imagine the surface of the water from below — sunlight, the ripples, the shadows of the trees, a sudden disturbance. As a fish you hear the splash of a June Bug before you see it. You follow the vibrations in the water that lead you, and your fellow denizen of the deep, to the thrashing beetle. The creature's silhouette heading for shore, doing its best at the beetle stroke, in an instant becomes fish grits. You, the fish, feel the hard shell crunch in your mouth and then the fluttering of wings in your stomach, and finalize the whole experience with an intoxicated grin and a cheerful wagging of your dorsal membrane.

Java

With a stoked fire
the soot-black billy starts to talk
and we listen to its' words of wisdom
before transforming the clear water into mud

Steam rising
from the coffee mug
creates a diffusion
in which all is possible
and life is simplified
into realistic
sips

Fishing is made up of secrets. Lots of fish secrets and human secrets that change secretly throughout the day. The most closely guarded secrets are the secluded locations of proven ponds and bends in a hidden river. Then come the secret flies, secret line, and disguised casts for every new ripple, boulder, and unknown beaver lodge. And the secret girlfriends with fisherman fathers who unknowingly mutter, after consuming healthy volumes of clever-juice, inherited information passed down through generations about the hard-to-reach magic pools. Fish secrets are born to be told. What good is a secret if you're the only one who knows it. The line that John Prine wrote, "I don't think that you know, that I think you don't know," all makes sense when you're searching for speckles.

Wooly Bugger? Cat's Whiskers? Black Booby? Marabou Bastard? Natural Zonker? Blue Zulu? Goat's Toe? Sam Slick?
Drowning Daddy? Mr. Nasty? Dogsbody? Klinkenhammer Special? Rat-Faxed McDougal?
Gord Carl reaches out with spiritual desires for the elusive Speckle.

Dave and I were floating downstream towards the ripples in the distance. Sitting in the bow of an old cedar-canvas canoe Dave was delivering good air time on the 6-weight line, seeing the landing, watching for the rise, waiting for the gulp, the tug, and the commotion of the reel as line is taken out — but no luck this time. The canoe reached the shoreline and we pulled it up onto the pebbled grade at the start of the portage. Dave straddled the bow, facing backward with his feet onshore to steady the canoe while I unloaded the packs, wanigan, day packs, and assorted loose trinkets. After losing the best two-out-of-three at throwing fingers, Dave had to portage the canoe, double back for the packs, and then a third time for the wanigan and leftovers while I got to creep along the 650 yards of rocky, wooded shoreline.

Quite a distance downstream I finally encounter the "glory hole." A pool that eddies out of the moving water and is half hidden behind a ridge of large boulders. I'm sure the water is boiling with fish. My heart doublebeats. I tie one of Dave's homemade mystic gems of feather and thread to the leader and wrist flip it into the breeze. Back and forth, marooned only by mono-filament, the fly reaches greater distances with every *whip-whoosh* of rod and line. It remains airborne while it floats over the pool for a split

second, and then it is gone again as the sun illuminates the sweeping curves of the hollow line. I feel the tug even before I see the circular ripples on the smooth pool in front of me. No wonder! The reckless line has hooked the cedar tree behind and upstream. The unexpected grab interrupts the poetic rhythm of hand and arm, and swings my body towards the moving water. Both feet glide off the algae-covered rock that was keeping me secure in the river. With arms outstretched and scrambling for balance, I go down. I hear the collision of round rocks hitting each other underwater. The water is cold because trout like cold water. I do everything possible to protect the rod. It happens quickly, but the waders still fill up because I forgot to tighten the belt. I crawl out of the water and stand up.

Like every good fisherman, I look around to make sure no one was watching. I'm wet, cold, humbled and still hooked up there in the trees somewhere. Underwater vibrations and quakes have entered into the flat water pool and have spooked all the fish. You just know the trout have gone into hiding because they're smart enough to realize something alien and clumsy is upstream. Even the chubb are in concealment, with wide eyes and fins quietly strumming the water, waiting in a darker shadow of a shadow.

When I arrive at the end of the portage the canoe is fully loaded and pointing towards another bend. Dave notices that I am wet and don't have any fish, but he pretends not to notice. Between the two of us, he's the one who most certainly knows how to catch these guys, and I feel as though I've wasted a beautiful stretch of river

As essential as trout and Wooly Buggers may seem for everlasting happiness, just being in a canoe with a companion and traveling through the wilderness surrounded by all this beauty makes up for the scarcity of the Speckled One. Dave is again in the bow, and as we glide slowly downstream, he looks back over his shoulder as if he is giving me the complete hairy-eyeball, then turns forward and selects a fly. A secret fly. He ties it on quickly and I'm sure he kisses it twice before dropping it into the water. Droplets mist off the line with each aerial S-turn. The coils of line in the canoe decrease in number with every forward reach of the rod. With eyes focused, and the last whiplash of line racing for the smooth bend forty feet in front of the canoe, he lets the fly plop on top of the water. The two of us sit still and wait for reluctant Speckies; worshippers, a holy quest, fishseekers with spiritual desires for its flesh and beauty. Suddenly the surface implodes. The fly disappears and the shrill sound of outgoing line has me scratching my bug-bitten head.

Don Standfield

THE MARINE
FOOD CHAIN
IN ACTION

Taking their cue from the fins, gulls descended on the spot, whirling and stabbing at some feed just beneath the surface. I had the binoculars pressed to my eyes, trying to see what they were eating, when I felt something bumping the canoe. Thinking I had drifted against the kelp, I paid no attention. But when the bump-bump-bump became more insistent, I looked over the side, and my stomach clenched. Beneath me was an undulating mass of thousands upon thousands of sharks, densely packed from the surface for as far down as I could see into the depths. Swimming with sinuous, hypnotic grace, they glided over and under and around one another, never touching and never stopping. They possessed a sinister kind of beauty: their bodies velvety dove grey with fins and tails edged in dusky chalk, and backs longitudinally stippled by parallel rows of white stars. I resisted an urge to reach out and stroke their flanks; spines stood up behind their dorsal and adipose fins, and the dogfish's teeth, I knew, could slice a fish as cleanly as a scalpel. Even the touch of their sandpaper skin provokes a shiver like the screech of steel on glass.

I pushed ahead into the feeding mass, sending the gulls wheeling overhead. The water was a mauve soup of slender, inch-long organisms, swimming in short bursts just beneath the surface. In the brim of my hat, which I used to scoop a few out, they appeared insubstantial as water, except for a scarlet thread of internal organs and a pair of pinpoint black eyes. They were krill, a species of planktonic crustaceans.

The dogfish fed all around me, swimming back and forth through the mauve cloud with their mouths open, for all the world like baleen whales.

Michael Poole, *Ragged Islands*

Going Bump in the Night

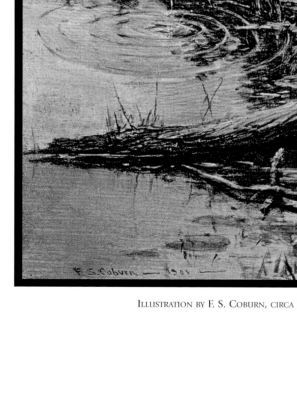

ILLUSTRATION BY F. S. COBURN, CIRCA 1900.

Sleep at last — or so I thought. No sooner had I closed my eyes than a loud thumping broke out down by the lake. Some varmint was using one of our canoes for a bass drum! Grabbing tennis shoes, flashlight, and an aspen shillelagh, I rushed to the boats.

Two bull moose with lowered antlers were facing each other; one shiny red canoe separated the snorting, black behemoths. The two opponents preferred to stand and argue and kick the aluminum craft rather than move the eight feet either way to more adequate grounds for combat. They ignored me and my flashlight, probably because neither moose dared take his eyes of the other for so much as a side glance, out of respect for a possible ramming from his opponent's eighty-five-pound rack of antlers. Bull moose possess the heaviest horns in the animal kingdom.

My own panic grew with each passing moment lest one of the 2000-pound monsters suddenly step inside the canoe and pierce the hull with a sharp, splayed hoof. I couldn't just crouch there behind a tree and witness the destruction of a canoe. Suddenly remembering that my father had once said that a moose is afraid of nothing but fire, I rushed back up hill to camp, grabbed some matches and a paper sack and returned to the battlefield. Neither moose had budged an inch, and both were still thumping the canoe. Placing a small stone in the bottom of the sack, I ignited the dry paper and tossed it between the hind legs of the nearest animal. The hotfoot broke up the stalemate, but the canoe's custom paint job was pocked and dented.

Robert Leslie, *Read the Wild Water*, 1966
A description of Leslie's trip
leading nine teenaged boys down the Green River.

Moose sightings are still one of the highlights of a northern trip.
Since 1900, some 267,849 pituitarily supercharged North American males have been affectionately nicknamed Moose.

Eating My Hat

Friday morning was warm and bright. It seemed wonderful to be having so much fine weather in Labrador, and not a fly or mosquito as yet. The one nuisance we had met was mice or lemmings. They had been busy with my hat in the night, and when I came to put it on that morning I found there was a hole eaten in the crown and a meal or two taken out of the brim. There seemed to be thousands of them, and they ran squealing about everywhere, great fat fellows, some of them as big as grey squirrels. The ground was so perforated with their holes that it reminded one of porous plaster.

Mina Hubbard, *A Woman's Way Through Unknown Labrador*

Some say the motivation behind the vigorous northern fur trade had little to do with European fashion demands.

A shore lunch of tender trout.

What Solitudes recording artists do when not on tour.
A common loon enters the shallows looking for deeper water and a fish breakfast.

Nightfall

orange moon

rises

distant thunder sky booming

a loon call echoes ...

softly

and

slowly.

moisture hangs

heavy

in the

air.

rain looms.

silence surrounds

the last tent

murmurings

of the day.

TODD BARR

WRITTEN ON DAY 34

OF A 50-DAY CANOE TRIP

KIDNAPPED

We picked up our fourth man in a bar in Buffalo late one September night. With four we could travel better in two canoes, instead of packing three big guys into one canoe. So, drunken Bob, who was celebrating the end of a four-year hitch in the U.S. Navy, was our answer. He stated, with plastered positiveness, that he had always dreamed of going on a canoe trip, a yearning which qualified him for our expedition, drunk or sober.

Bob woke up in the back seat of our car, loaded to its gunwales with packsacks and paddles, around Barrie, halfway to Algonquin Park. His only baggage was a one-hundred-pound hangover and breath that would bring a bull moose to his knees. Kidnapped, he was on his way to the handsome Algonquin waters for a two-week fall canoe trip.

We reintroduced ourselves, stopped to rig up Bob with boots and jacket and our personal surplus wear, including a hat which would stop traffic in the central aisle of an Ontario men's beverage room.

Bob learned the bow stroke fast and portaged well. He got fully into the physical part of the canoe trip, loving the wild waters and woods, and getting along just fine with his new friends of the bush.

Bob's problem didn't occur until later, in the second week, after the young rutty bull moose almost trampled us early one snowy morning as we lay in our sleeping bags. He accepted with good spirit the rain that dumped on us the first night out, a deluge that reduced the concept of tarp protection to no protection at all. No problem yet.

Fact is, he loved the bullshit we pulled on Mic up on the Petawawa just south of Catfish. When Jeff was casting his flyrod into the black-green curlbacks just off the campsite, he noticed that the fool's fish (red dace overblown to bass size) would lazily take a wet fly. By jigging around the tip of the flyrod, Jeff could make the fightless fish look like they were battling at Trafalgar, especially when he started yelling excitedly, "SPECKLES!" Maybe it wasn't fair, because Mic was one of these guys who is in a continual state of desperate hunger and would eat the worst thing in the world and then suck around for seconds. Big Swifty, who was just about to blow the whole production by busting out with the world's dumbest natural science observation, (i.e. "Those aren't speckles"), caught the finger-over-the-lips signal for silence and fell into line. Bob, just like Mic, couldn't tell a speckle from a ham sandwich, so he was safe.

Well, no guff, Mic cooked up and devoured all twelve of the tasteless river slums as we all winked at each other. Mic was a little put out later when he realized he'd been duped. We were on Philip Lake one evening and every species in the park was coming out to show itself off — moose, deer, a bear, ducks, geese. A real seventeen-inch speckle took a spoon in the late sunset and ended up in a fry pan.

It was after all this bunch of fun and bush happening, which only life on the outside can provide for the human soul, that Bob's problem landed on us. Wolves. They were howling, all right, and travelling in a pack formed in the crispy fall weather of late September. They howled as they got closer and closer, as we were laid out like herring in our sleeping bags under our tarp with no walls between us and the "toothy killers." Bob was dealing with the certainty that he would be killed first and eaten by the Algonquin Park wolves — simple as that — killed and eaten. God, we tried to convince him that they wouldn't do it — never have done it — not in one hundred years. Specifically, it was detailed to him that no case histories exist in Algonquin Park wherein a wolf even attacked, let alone killed, a human being. Done! The four of us lay symmetrically quiet after the strong reassurance — but only for a short while, when Bob said, "Yeah, we know that — but do they?"

Jeff Miller, artist, conservationist, paddler

THE MYSTICAL SIDE
OF CANOE TRAVEL

Misshipeshu, serpents and a canoe at Agawa Rock, Lake Superior.

MISSHIPESHU, THE WATER GOD

My ancestor, my great-great-grandfather four generations ago, whose name was Little Grouse, had a medicine dream concerning an offering rock where the water demigod Misshipeshu, in the form of a huge cat, spoke to him and advised him to put on the rock a sacred sign made out of onaman, the Ojibway sacred sand. It was in the summer, and the water demigod helped my great-great-grandfather to put its sign on the walls of the cliffs. From then on, until thirty years ago, Indians of that area offered gifts to Misshipeshu.

In those days only the Ojibway Indians were at Lake Nipigon, there was no white man and everything was quiet. Maybe this is the main reason all water beings were seen so freely. But when the white men came and brought with them fish nets, motorboats, airplanes and railroads, these beings, the Ojibway believe, moved to a quieter place. Ojibway Indians of Lake Nipigon had an offering rock erected to this huge cat. Offerings of copper pails were thrown into the water and black dogs as well as white dogs, decorated in the very best, were offered alive to the water god for it to eat. In the time of the early traders, traps, guns and firewater, as well as great amounts of tobacco, were also put into the water. This was done once a year around June, in order not to offend the water god and to bring good luck to all those who believed in these offerings. Canoes formed a circle at the offering rock, as these rites took place on the water.

This huge cat is believed by the Ojibway to be white in colour, with horns, and very powerful. It is believed to live in the water but why a cat lives in the water, or where it lived, is not known. There is another big demigod of the same cat family who was considered very evil, but was a spirit. If anyone dreamed of this big water demigod at the time of fasting it was believed to bring misfortune, not to the dreamer but to his children. For this cat had to be pleased; it lived on human flesh or souls, but also accepted offerings of white pups about six months old to replace human souls. These offerings, however, were made very seldom, for this demigod was never demanding.

This big water god, or spirit, knew both good and evil. It all depended on what kind of nature an Indian had. If he were good then he would have the power to do good. If he were bad then he was given power to do bad. But the true water god, the white one in colour, always brought good luck to all who respected him....

At Lake Superior...this legend was told to me by Luke Nanakonagos. An Indian family was travelling one summer near the area called Agawa Rock. On one of the beaches the Ojibway Indian said to his wife, "Let us make a fire, to eat." They left for the bush, the woman to get wood, the man for bark, leaving their only child, wrapped in a tikinagan, or carrier, near the canoe, although the old-time Ojibway feared Lake Superior.

On returning they found their baby gone. When they looked at the sand, they saw Misshipeshu's footprints. The tracks were seen leading into the water, with the baby. The couple did not know what to do. Finally the man spoke, "I will call on my protectors, the birds of thunder, to come to our help. Although we shall not see our child again, I will do what I can through the help of my protectors. Let us now go under the canoe," and then he started to play his drum.

In about half an hour the thunderbirds, or thunderstorm, arrived in that area. The lightning began to pour on a mountain close by and it got dark. For two hours the storm lasted. Misshipeshu tried to hide but lightning fell all over the place and he was killed. Then the rain and lightning ceased, the skies cleared and the sun shone again. On the waters of Lake Superior, by the shore, an empty cradle was seen floating and beside it two small dead cubs. So ends this legend.

Norval Morrisseau, *Legends of My People*

Tobacco Offerings at Chaudière Falls, June 1613

After having carried their canoes below the falls, they get together in one place, where one of them, with a wooden plate, takes up a collection, and each one of them puts into this place a piece of tobacco. The collection made, the plate is put into the middle of the band, and all dance around it, singing in their fashion; then one of the chiefs makes a speech, showing that for a long time they have been accustomed to make this offering, and that by this means they are guaranteed against their enemies; that otherwise misfortune would befall them... That done, the speaker takes the plate and goes and throws the tobacco into the middle of the cauldron, and they raise a great cry all together. These people are so superstitious that they do not expect to have a good journey if they have not had this ceremony in this place, for their enemies await them in this passage, not daring to advance farther because of the bad trails; and sometimes they surprise them there.

Samuel de Champlain, *The Voyages and Explorations of Samuel de Champlain 1604–16*

At the Height of Land

A few days and some fifty miles beyond Grand Portage, the northwest route crossed the Hauteur de Terre. This Height of Land was more than a few acres of scrub trees and rock where all the streams behind the westbound canoes flowed to the Great Lakes and all those ahead to the vague, remote north. For the streams flowing into Lake Superior flowed homeward for each white man. No matter how he had longed for adventure, at the Height of Land he felt a swift, overwhelming panic, part homesickness and part apprehension.

Perhaps it was because the Height of Land was more than geography — it was a Rubicon. A ceremony marked each man's first crossing, as it is marked at the equator. From boyhood each voyageur had heard of this ceremony until it became a legend. Back on his father's farm along the St. Lawrence, or more likely in his mother's warm kitchen, old hands had pictured their own moments of excitement and panic during this unforgettable moment of their first trip to the interior. In a sense they were prepared for it. Young McGillivray had no such background.

Even before the canoes left Lachine the voyageurs as well as the bourgeois had made a point of preparing Mr. McTavish's nephew for the ordeal. They had hoped he would be able to measure up to the initiation. "Some men..." they commenced to tell him of this man or that — but always they broke off before they divulged the frailties of his predecessors. By the time his own fateful day arrived, William McGillivray was steadying himself for an ordeal

Palm Sunday.
Steve Terljhan celebrates a successful crossing.

equal to that of a young Indian facing the rites of manhood.

The east-flowing streams had dwindled. Canoes and packs and kegs had been carried to the first west-flowing water when the brigade paused at the far edge of the rocky little plateau, covered with sparse clumps of bush. The stream where they would refloat the canoes was little more than a creek of fast water, riffled as much by wind as by current, and here and there shaded by a few scrub cedar.

McGillivray had become accustomed to the noise of a fur-brigade party; the continual profane banter and singing of the voyageurs at the carrying-places, and the quieter talk of the clerks and bourgeois. The sudden, dramatic silence was in itself a shock. About him stood the men of the entire brigade, doing nothing in broad daylight. As if it had all been rehearsed many times, the guide who had made the most trips to the northwest, a man not over thirty, stepped forward, unsheathing his hunting knife from his belt. A few paces from the tyro, and beside a clump of cedar, he paused to examine the blade of the knife. Not satisfied, he sharpened the blade slowly and carefully, testing it on the hairs of his weathered wrist. McGillivray watched the steel cut through one of the stiff hairs as though it were butter. Still with the air of detachment, the guide, now very much master of ceremonies, looked about him at the scrub cedar, selected and cut off a bough with a single slash of the knife. Only then did he address the initiate, McGillivray, ordering him to a low spot beside the stream. In a voice that rang out across the little plateau he commanded: "Kneel!"

McGillivray had doffed his cap. Now he dropped to his knees. Suddenly his head and shoulders were drenched with cold water, dipped from the stream with the cedar bough. The guide commanded him to repeat the ancient two-fold promise. Keeping his voice as firm as he could, McGillivray swore in French never to permit a new-comer to pass the Height of Land without a similar ceremony — and never to kiss a voyageur's wife without her permission.

Someone fired a shot into the air as he scrambled to his feet. Every man present shook his hand, thumped him on the back, cried out congratulations and called for a drink to toast the newly initiated northman.

The toast was the real reason for the ceremony, some said. But even then William McGillivray sensed that there was much more to it. Already he realized that only a few hundred men made the long, dangerous trip each year. He felt something of the deep emotion behind each northman's proud boast: "Je suis un homme du nord!"

Now he, too, was a northman.

Marjorie Wilkins Campbell, *The North West Company*

Mamaygwessey on Dipper Lake

Rainbow to windward, foul fall the day; rainbow to leeward, damp runs away.

No sooner had we left the fireplace than Elliott yelled: "A canoe is gone!" We rushed to the ledge where we had placed the three canoes so carefully the night before, with their bows all pointing up hill and into the wind. There were only two. I should have taken a turn with the bow lines around a boulder or a tree, but I had been so sure that the pocket they rested in would protect them. Once I lost a canoe, years ago, and had to swim half a mile to the shore. We were in serious trouble, and the expedition was barely underway! Six men could not possibly travel through storms and rapids in two canoes with any degree of comfort or safety.

Omond wasted no time on self-recrimination. He got out the glasses and scanned the far shore a mile away. The white-capped waves were high now and rolling across the channel. If by some chance the canoe had been blown off the ledge, it would drift over there, but in those waves it could not last long against the cliffs. He studied the shoreline, watching the spray dash high against the rocks, then steadied on a point to one side of the steepest shore. "I see something," he said. "Might be it." He handed the glasses to me.

A tiny gray shape — the canoe without a doubt — was bouncing gently against a clump of willow and birch to one side of the cliff. Up and down in the waves it moved, caught by the bushes and seemingly held there. We would have to hurry if we were to save it. Elliott, Omond, Tony, and Denis took off immediately in one canoe, and I watched as they hit the open water and all but disappeared in the troughs.

What good fortune made the canoe land against those bushes instead of the rocks we would never know. How the wind could lift it off without a sound and with no paint left anywhere was also a mystery. Not until we learned about the Mamaygwessey did we know the truth.

The voyageurs were now at the cliff, holding onto the empty canoe in the willows. For a moment they disappeared and all I could see was spray and confusion, then suddenly the two canoes broke away and were fighting the waves on the way back. It took half an hour for them to come across the channel and everyone was drenched. The stray canoe was unscratched, two of its three paddles still inside and not a drop of water had been shipped. Ten feet to the north and it would have been pounded against the cliff. A little later Elliott found the third paddle floating just below the fireplace. How it had been thrown out was also part of the mystery....

Moody told us about the Mamaygwessey, the little men with round heads, no noses, long spidery arms and legs with six fingers and six toes, whose likenesses we had seen among the pictographs of Black Bear Island Lake.

"These little creatures," he explained, "live usually in the rocks of rapids and when canoes come through, they delight in grasping the paddles or gunwales and when a canoe tips over, their shrieks of delight can be heard above the noise of the rapids.

When we told him what happened to our canoe on Dipper Lake, how it had blown off a rock without a trace or taking any water, he laughed aloud.

"That's exactly the way they would do it," he said. "Not a sound or a mark anywhere. And you can be sure they saw to it that the canoe didn't smash itself to pieces against the cliff, but bounced around against those willows. You see there's no real mischief in their antics, just good clean fun."

Sigurd Olson, *The Lonely Land*

We need the tonic of Wilderness. – to wade sometimes in marshes where the bittern and the meadow-hen lurk, and hear the booming of the snipe: to smell the whispering sedge where only some wilder and more solitary fowl builds her nest. and the mink crawls with its belly close to the ground.

Henry David Thoreau, *Walden*

THE WILBERFORCE FALLS AFFAIR

The couple stood at a pulpit made of canoe paddles. The bride's full-length satin wedding dress with a flowing train and ermine trim obscured the green Wellies on her feet. The groom wore a crisp white shirt with red bow tie and cummerbund, and the legs of his freshly washed wool trousers were tucked into the leather uppers of his L.L. Bean Maine hunting shoes. The air was consumed by the song of Wilberforce Falls of the Hood River, Northwest Territories.

Welcome to the wedding of Cliff Jacobson and Susie Harings.

It was a setting befitting of a couple who met through canoeing. Susie, a middle school teacher from River Falls, Wisconsin, and Cliff, a teacher, writer, wilderness guide, became friends during trips with the Minnesota Canoe Association. Their marriage took place in August 1992.

But Susie Harings didn't agree to marry Cliff Jacobson until she knew the wedding would be yet another grand adventure. And like most weddings, there were hitches to getting hitched.

Cliff's summer plans revolved around a canoe trip on Hood River in the Northwest Territories, where he would guide a gang of nine men down the remote Arctic waterway. Wilberforce Falls — an awesome cataract that drops 160 feet through a three-mile canyon — would be

the perfect wedding site. But there was no room for his fiancée: paying customers first, love 'n' matrimony second.

Luckily a cancellation allowed Susie to join the trip. That didn't bother her a bit, even when she discovered that her bridesmaid would be a man.

Cliff had arranged to fly to the Hood from Yellowknife, Northwest Territories, but to get there from River Falls, Wisconsin, the crew drove 2,311 miles, for 46 hours non-stop. Beyond Yellowknife the pavement stops at the Mackenzie River. After that, it's dust, road oil, and fist-sized gravel.

For Cliff and Susie, business in Yellowknife included certifying Charles LeFevere to be their "marriage commissioner." In sparsely populated Northwest Territories, people — especially ministers — are rare above the tree line. That's why there are marriage commissioners.

Twin Otter Air Tindi floatplanes flew the crew and gear from Yellowknife to the quiet bay above the first rapid on the Hood River. As the transport took off, Cliff noticed something was missing. "Where's the wedding pack?" he called. Dead silence.

"O.K., you guys, who hid the wedding pack? It's not funny," yelled Susie. Again, no answer. The white canvas Duluth pack, which contained all their wedding accoutrements, was either on the disappearing plane or 300 air-miles away.

"I can't get married without my dress and cake! I won't be married without my dress," Susie cried hysterically. "I won't! I won't! I won't!"

Charging grizzly and foot-stomping muskox cannot match the fury of a whining woman on the tundra. Rain, rapids, portages, and the excitement of the tundra encouraged her perspective. By the time the first camp was pitched, the loss was a distant reality.

The crew had no sooner settled into the comfort of their first hot toddy when a plane zoomed in, banked a turn and jettisoned what? The wedding pack!

Ten days later, on August 12, the wedding party arrived at Wilberforce Falls, a spectacular highlight of the north. The normally thundering cascade was a picturesque dry coliseum of balconies and caves. Breathtaking views encompass hundreds of miles of uninhabited tundra, a river valley of immense proportions, and the Arctic Ocean.

Unbeknownst to the bride and groom, a secret extravaganza had been prepared. Bridesmaid Brad Bjorklund had scooped out a cathedral-like "chapel of the blue dome" where Susie was to be hidden from view until the wedding march, played from a tiny music box, announced her entrance. The guests were formal in tuxedo t-shirts. Also witnessing the event were two Canadian geologists the crew had met at an abandoned mine along the river and invited to the wedding.

Clad in a flowing black robe, Charlie "His Excellency" LeFevere approached the pulpit, a tripod of canoe paddles. Cliff appeared, freshly clad and shaven, accompanied by best man Biff Kummer, who nervously clutched the well-traveled ring. Susie, escorted by bridesmaid Brad, carried a bouquet of dried Wisconsin and fresh tundra flowers. She stepped in time down the water-worn aisle to "Here Comes the Bride."

Just before the vows were taken, a huge raven, jet black and preened, flew into the cathedral and perched on a flat rock, a dozen feet away. Unafraid, the bird just stood and watched. As the ceremony began, the raven flew casually away and seconds later, a white gull took his spot. Everyone was touched by this favorable omen of raven magic. The Indian spirit book, *Medicine Cards*, by Jamie Sams and David Carson, explains: "Raven is the messenger that carries all energy flows of ceremonial magic between the ceremony itself and the intended destination... It is the power of the unknown at work, and something special is about to happen."

To Cliff, the meaning was clear: "It meant our union was blessed by my late wife, Sharon," he said. Sharon had died suddenly in December 1990.

The ceremony ended with a traditional kiss near the top of the world. At the reception site, within yards of the thundering falls, a feast was spread out on a space blanket. Smoked oysters, kippered herring, pepperoni and sardines; nuts, mints and rich chocolate bars. In the center of it all was a white, richly frosted, two layer cake with a plastic wedding couple on top, survivors of the Air Tindi drop.

As Cliff poured the wedding cognac, the geologists strolled forward bearing a large box wrapped in newspaper and bound with orange surveying ribbon. "It was all we could come up with on such short notice," said the elder man.

Susie tore open the box. "It's a toaster, a real toaster!" she screamed in disbelief. Sure enough, it was a toaster, and a four-slice model, to boot.

As the couple walked to the pinnacle of the falls for their wedding portrait, a plane zoomed out of nowhere and buzzed the falls, just clearing its upper ledge. It wagged a salute and turned toward Yellowknife. Later, Cliff learned it was his friend Bob Dannert, en route home from a trip down the Simpson River.

"I could see it all," Bob said later. "The white dress, red cummerbund, and gourmet spread. By the way, was that really a toaster?"

Boo Turner and Cliff Jacobson,
Canoe magazine

MYSTERY OF THE BARRENS

We had picked this site because the map indicated an "astronomical monument" nearby, a survey point left by a government team 20 years before. Though we couldn't find that marker, we did discover a stranger monument of sorts, seemingly more related to astronomy.

On a small point near our campsite were several unnatural looking rock formations. Four slender pillars of rock stood in a dead straight line. Each pillar, three feet high, was firmly bedded in a cluster of smaller rocks around the base. The line of stone obelisks, reminiscent of some druid cromlech, was oriented northwest-southeast. What did it represent? Obviously it had been erected by men. But when? How long ago? No one, in the journals of previous Back River travellers, had mentioned the stone formation. Had none of our twentieth-century predecessors, not perhaps even George Back himself, stopped at this point?

At sunset we gathered around the point as if compelled by some ancient rite. Watching the sun slip below the horizon to the northwest, the stone pillars extended a line almost directly into the sunset. The compass bearing of sunset changes slightly each night, as the sun's position relative to the earth moves north or south. As winter approaches, the sun sets slightly farther south (about one degree at this latitude) on each successive evening. Hasty calculations showed that in three nights' time, July 31, the sun would set directly along the line of these stone pillars. What could this mean? Our imaginations sprinted.

Years ago, the coastal Inuit from Bathurst Inlet, less than a hundred miles to the north-northwest, could have moved inland to Beechey Lake for the caribou hunt. The area was traditionally well populated with caribou during the summer. We knew that. If such were the case, if this were a seasonal hunting ground, the Inuit would be wary enough to head home in time to beat winter's fury on the Barrens. A series of pillars such as we had found could be their time-piece. When the sun set

Tent circle remnants. Evidence of the true tent dwellers.

along that line, as the days began to shorten near summer's end, it was time to collect together the spoils of the hunt and remove to the coast for winter. Had we found a marker from ages past? Or did it hold some other mystical secret?

Looking along the line of pillars the other way, we faced the expanse of Beechey Lake, disappearing over the southeastern horizon. It was easy for us to make this association. But in spring, with the lake still frozen and the Barrens covered with a vast blanket of snow, perhaps these markers could provide a valuable clue as to the river's direction. This region was between those historically occupied by Indians and Inuit, respectively to the south and north. They had come here only to hunt. It was a

source of pride to these native peoples to excel in their local knowledge of the country. Back himself had said that there was an "instinct which will guide an Indian through mazes of the darkest and most tangled forest." But here, at Beechey Lake, they might not be comfortable. Their normal sense of direction might well require the assistance of these few stone markers.

As we sat on the shore of the lake, we wondered. The full moon rose in the southeastern sky. The air seemed full of mystery. We had stopped to find an astronomical monument. Had we instead found an unknown monument to a past civilization?

David Pelly, *Expedition*

The only true time which a man can properly call his own, is that which he has all to himself:
the rest, though in some sense he may be said to live it, is other people's time, not his.

ENGLISH ESSAYIST CHARLES LAMB

At Denison Falls

The place that I really wanted to get to was Denison Falls, partly because it was one of Bill's favorite places and partly because it had this mystique that had been built up over the years. So off I went, tracking up the Dog River, with my Wellies on. When it got too hard to track, I started simply wading up the river with the canoe. In no time, I was wet to my knees. I took my stuff out of my pants pockets and put it in my shirt pockets. Before long, I was wet to the waist... absolutely soaking wet, fumbling in the water, deathly afraid that I was going to wreck this canoe, this museum specimen that Joyce Mason had entrusted me with.

Anyway, I got up to what I thought was the place, soaking wet and a little disappointed. I thought, "Boy, Denison Falls isn't that great. Maybe, like Bill, it looks bigger in movies." It was really hot and I was soaked, so I took off my wet things and I laid them out on this beautiful gray rock. I took off my socks, and my pants, and my shirt, and then I went exploring a little bit.

To the right of the falls I noticed this great big rope, a kind of hawser, dangling down. Using this rope, I climbed straight up this rock, thinking that Denison Falls had been a big let-down and that I had gone to an awful lot of bother to see nothing very much at all. At the top of the rock, a trail led further up the river.

I was going along the trail, looking at the beautiful mountain ash berries that were there, when all of a sudden, I think I tasted it first, this sweet spindrift that sort of floated through the air. And as I got a little bit closer, I could feel the ground resonating, vibrating. What happens is, you cut the corner on the gorge and you end up coming out high on the gorge, looking right out across from Denison Falls. You are confronted by a spectacle that sucks the wind right out of you, this tumult of water and rock that Bill had spoken about. Denison Falls. I just stood there, breathing this beautifully delicious, sweet, wet air. The water was low at the time, and I just spent the afternoon playing around here, wandering up and down, sitting, watching what was going on, mesmerized at times by the patterning of the water.

For those of you that travel, let this be a warning. The large skies and stark beauty of these northern places can move and challenge you as gently, as insistently, as completely as the warmest and most profound of lovers. It truly becomes possible to have a love affair with the land. As for us, we all had a difficult time returning, and part of each of us probably never will.

Jesse Ford

Human...nature.
Diane Bald holds onto memories with pastel and paper
before the rest of the trip wakes up.

Eventually, I made my way back down to where my stuff was drying, and two things linger in my memory as being a little bit spooky. One was a butterfly that was lingering all around my stuff. Maybe there was some food on my pants, I don't know. But it was flying all around and it was noticeable enough that I eventually took a couple of photographs of it as it sat on my belt. Then I put my pants back on, put my shirt on, and I walked down the rock to pick up my socks — two great big, red work socks. But there was only one there. I looked all around. There was no wind. There were no birds. The sock appeared to have disappeared into thin air.

To this day, I am convinced that Bill Mason was sitting up in the woods somewhere, with my sock on a stick, killing himself laughing. *Big* joke. But I was totally spooked at that time, and even more so when I got back to Wawa. You know those printed paper placemats that they have in greasy-spoon restaurants along the Trans-Canada, the ones with all kinds of witticisms and useless advice? Well, as I sat down for a club sandwich and fries, having just come back from the Dog River, mine informed me that in China people think that the spirits of their dead inhabit butterflies.

Based on James Raffan's experiences while researching *Fire in the Bones*, his biography of Bill Mason. Mason, a filmmaker, artist, and expert canoeist, died in 1988. Bill's widow, Joyce, loaned her husband's 16-foot Chestnut Prospector to Raffan for this trip to one of Mason's most cherished spots on Lake Superior.

BONDS AND TRIP DYNAMICS

ALL YOU CAN EAT, 1823

The afternoon is most favorable for the voyage and this delay [adjustments to the canoe], created as it seem'd, by the Frenchmen, annoyed me very much. Satisfied however that they were exercising their best judgement, and well knowing that everything goes wrong when they are not permitted to be lords of the canoe & the portages, I did not interfere. It would have been fatal to all peace or comfort for a few days at least to have counteracted their plans for their darling canoe. Pride, self-will and obstinacy are virtues with the Canadian in many matters. As an instance, they had alarmed me on account of provisions. Fearing from their gluttony I should fall short, I put them upon rations & constant grumbling & discontent was the consequence. When secure of a supply I allowed them to help themselves, and they actually ate less, traveled farther, and were better-tempered animals for the change.

Major John Delafield surveying the disputed Canada–U. S. border in 1823.

LEONARD

He can speak fluent French, imitate a loon or Carol Burnett, start a fire in snow with one match after two days of rain, stand up and pole a loaded canoe through rapids, upstream or down. He can patch a gashed canoe with spruce pitch and strips of handkerchief, and produce pancakes as light as a whitecap. He calls the twigs and leaves that rattle down onto a tent at night "dry spills," and his red stocking cap a "bonnet." "I saw the last of the best of this country," Leonard says, and he probably did. Happily for us, he agreed to accompany Sam and me on a 92-mile canoe trip down the Allagash Wilderness Waterway, a protected chain of lakes and rivers.

Leonard has spent a lifetime in canoes — can build them, widen them, or lengthen them — but is mystified by the popularity of the sport of canoeing. "I don't see how anybody could get a thrill out of riding down the Allagash in a canoe," he says. While he was growing up, canoeing was not a form of recreation; it was simply the most practical way of getting around on the rivers and lakes of Maine....

Later Leonard told us of a young couple he had seen come through Chase's Carry a couple of years earlier. They were soaked, disgruntled·and unhappy, their gear all lost, their "little light canoe" damaged. Leonard said to the woman, "Next year when you come back, I expect you'll have a better canoe." "I'll have a better man, too," she snapped.

Ron Fisher, *Still Waters, White Waters*

Joseph Odjack at a portage on the Lake Nipissing River.

I like terra firma – the more firma, the less terra.
AMERICAN PLAYWRIGHT GEORGE S. KAUFMAN

TRIPPING WITH KIDS

At three months, she gurgled and squirmed, a gummy grin peeking out of her lifejacket cocoon. The bow was her universe. Nothing existed beyond the bond of our smiles; and as though she soaked up our tranquil mood, she fell asleep to the gentle rock of each stroke.

Two years old and she took it all in stride. She was completely at home in the woods. With those sturdy legs chugging beneath her tiny pack, the portages were lengthy explorations. "Self, self, self," she insisted when I offered my hand to help her over a log. The tiny details were the most important. A chipmunk's hole, pebbles on the shoreline, and a few chocolate chips in the raisins ... these were canoe trip's lasting memories. A giggling tumble among the sleeping bags was the best entertainment. We scrambled out of the tent to watch a moose cross our campsite. "Can I pat him?" she asked.

For the five year old, the mossy trunks hid super heroes; our tent was shelter from monsters he'd conjure up excitedly. How proud the little guy was of making a difference with his paddle, even though the spurts were interrupted by lily pad harvest and waterplay, streams pulsing through his fingers as he leaned over the gunwale. "When can we roast the marsh-

mallows? How much farther? Can I go swimming now? When will we see a bear? Why is the moon out in the day?" When, how, why, why, why? It was all new again.

Our eight-year-old companion was a busy "do-er." Little balsam twigs dipped in sap made boats. There was leech collecting at a beachy campsite. Sand was in the socks, bathing suit, hair, sleeping bag. Firebuilding was a favorite. "Let's make our campfires as fun every year as they are this year," he said. And then there was fishing, fishing, and more fishing. "Do you think we'll catch that huge trout this year?" And just before sleep overcame us on our campsite, "I think I'll come here every year and I'll pass this on to *my* children. This is the most beautiful place in the world."

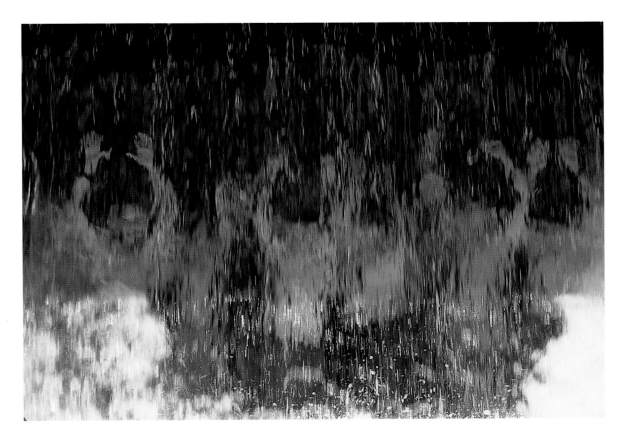

Creating a falls impression. The boys wash up
for their premeditated accidental arrival at a girls' camp just down the lake.

Everything had to be farther, faster, and bigger for the sixth graders. They absorbed every constellation's name that I could dredge from memory. We met on the portages as they sprinted back for second loads. They started taking a real interest in our route. "Let's take the long portage. We can climb the big hill to the lookout." Accomplishment was the name of the game, and beaming faces glowed with it.

Who wants to do much with older adults when they're fifteen? But canoe trips survived that awkward stage. Sulky, solemn teenagers of the city opened up around the campfire at night. There were passionate pronouncements on world issues and an ever-present sense of our earth's fragility. It was adult philosophy and madcap slapstick all bundled into one package of non-stop energy.

In later teens, the ones who are hooked eventually graduate to organizing their own trips with peers. It's a rare privilege to be allowed to read those trip journals:

"When I'm on canoe trip, I get this feeling of being at one with the surroundings and the people I'm with."

"There's this unique bond because you experience so much in a short time." "When everything is so beautiful, and I ask myself if I'm dreaming, I know I'm really *at home*. It's so hard to describe to someone who hasn't done this, but I think *this* is reality."

Young people have a way of changing the pace, of making things fresh by drawing attention to details and challenging us to squeeze every drop of enjoyment out of a day. We rarely traveled as far with young kids. We never lingered over coffee in the morning when we tripped with teenagers. But the experience was always enriched by the youthful sense of wonder brought to every precious moment.

Liz Lundell

IT CAN GET PRETTY HOT OUT THERE

Yes, I suppose I've seen an awful lot when it comes to guiding the city folk into the bush. Everytime I go to the lake country with these lads I come out with many a tale that makes for good smiles. I have as many stories as paddle dips in those lakes and rivers that I took 'em through. Here's one that you might have a hard time believing, but I still remember these fellas like it was yesterday.

I got a call from a so-called friend of mine, asking me to guide three fishermen that were coming up from the city, about four hundred miles south of here. A few nights before they were to arrive, I talked to them over the phone and made sure the days and times were the same as mine. They asked some unusual questions, but I answered them the best I could and then ended the conversation by suggesting they bring something special with them ... something we could all use on the trip or share on the campsite. Simple as that. I had hopes they would bring a variety of spirits or something along those lines.

Two days later the train pulled into the station and we all shook hands and talked about the weather and the fishing. I was pretty much ready to get moving, so we began loading their equipment into the back of the pickup truck. My throat was kinda scratchy, so I asked the first fella what he brought to share with the group. He said that he decided on some bottles of "French water" in case we got thirsty. Well, b'Jesus, the trip was for eight days and we would get good and goddamn thirsty that's for sure, but I told him we could drink the "Canadian water" right out of the lakes from underneath our canoes. I asked the second lad, hoping for more favorable results, and he told me that he had packed a large box of sardines. Indeed, this was a

This cottage sits on a chunk of rock four billion years old. *Billion.* Oldest rock on earth. The fishing started to get good about 400 million years ago. Fish dominated. Mind you, insects didn't come down the pike, so to speak, for another 50 million years, so you'd have wanted baitcasting gear, not your flyrod.

THORSEN SOLENBARG, RETIRED CONSERVATION OFFICER

better idea than the first fella's, but I shook my head in disbelief and thought about haulin' all those tins of foreign fish over the portages. I told him it never hurt to have some extra food in case the fish weren't in the mood for biting, but that I'd never been out on the lakes and skunked before. As we were talking, the third fella and the baggage handler pulled this huge burlap-covered object out of the train car and let 'er drop to the ground with a horrible crash. 'Twas clear enough to me that there was something strange going on and I just stood there scratchin' my head, half expecting to see something moving inside. The lad stood there with a proud little smirk on his face and began to undo the twine that was wrapped around the opening of the sack. Well, a guide could hardly believe what he was seeing. This fella, my client for the next week, told me that he had brought a car door along from the city ... so that if it got too hot out there we could roll down the window.

Yes, I've got lots of stories about guiding but not all of them have happy endings, and this would be one of them.

I've been a guide for most of my adult life and I wouldn't trade it for anyone else's. After spending time with a variety of men and women who make heaps of money in the city, I don't see the real happiness in 'em until they get out here on the lakes for a few days with a fishing rod in their hands. Next to my good looks, I guess it's the good air to breathe and the general lifestyle of the outdoors that has them all wanting to spend time with me. We all make choices in life, some bad and some good, but these people pay me to take 'em away from their life and into mine. That must tell you something right there. Most of the more experienced people that I guide enjoy sitting around the campfire listening to the stories just

as much as catching the fish, and the fish they do catch are admired for their size and beauty and then quickly released back into the lakes and rivers in which they were caught. The canoe trip experience has special meaning to the people who can slow down and grab onto that magic tonic that comes from the natural environment. They like the call of the loons in the morning and they determine the success of the day by the warmth of the sun on their faces and the friendships made on trip — instead of just hauling in trout. Whereas some of these young hot shots I guide, with all the latest fancy riggin', require catching their limit of fish each day and worry about the other guy hooking a bigger one. They don't feel the pure clean energy at the end of their line or the beauty of each fish as it gets closer to the canoe. I'm convinced that some of them don't even realize that this graceful creature is actually alive and fighting for its life. It's tough for me to watch, this lack of respect and appreciation. They miss so much because of the constant need to compete, and it has never ever made any sense to me. I suppose the competitive nature might keep them alive in the city, but it's going to kill 'em out here. A fella by the name of William James wrote: "Lives based on having are less free than lives based on either doing or being." A guide friend of mine told me this years ago and I believe in it completely. It takes a few days and some clever thinking on my part but I can gradually turn these young lads around and get them to relax long enough to see what the bush has to offer. Those are the people who I enjoy teaching, from that point on, and they usually come back year after year, eventually bringing their sons and daughters and wives with them. After guiding the same clients for several trips we become friends with a mutual respect for the bush and appreciation for the fish ...

and that's when I decide it's time to take them to those secret spots. To the small lakes and river bends where the fish have been known to jump out onto the shoreline and chase down an unsuspecting raccoon or porcupine.

There is great pleasure in traveling and living in the bush. There are great rewards in the camaraderie when you work together as a team to move the trip over a long portage or paddle the canoes into a heavy headwind on a big lake. After more than fifty-five years of guiding I continue to get great satisfaction from the clients who are able to leave the city mentality behind and truly feel the natural world. Let me read you something out of a book by Wendell Berry: "And the world cannot be discovered by a journey of miles, no matter how long, but only by a spiritual journey, a journey of one inch, very arduous and humbling and joyful, by which we arrive at the ground at our feet, and learn to be home." I suppose it would surprise a lot of people if they knew an old man in the bush read stuff like this, but it all makes so much sense to me. Being a guide these days is a lot more than just tying flies or removing hooks from the lips of fish. We are teachers educating our students through real-life experiences about the natural world — a world which is full of miracle animals, little flowers, huge trees, and beautiful fish in beautiful waters. All of these should be appreciated and given great respect. And believe me this is where we best belong if we behave. This is certainly where I belong. The old feeling that trout only live in beautiful places is true, but all will quickly be lost if we don't come to realize the urgent need for education, which in-turn naturally becomes preservation.

Okay, enough of my sermons. I should take you down the lake fishing. Just off that far point, the one with the three gnarled pines on it, is a magical hole clogged with trout. When you lean over the canoe and look down through the water you can barely make out a rusty square shape with a large opening in the middle of it where the fish love to hang out and flutter their fins. Even on the hottest day, in the middle of summer, the water seems to be so much cooler there than any other place on the lake. We can thank one of my fisherman clients for donating that "urban miracle."

Sammy Henson, guide, conservationist, storyteller

How Solitude Can Reveal the Meaning of Life

Canada's guru of canoeing, the late Bill Mason, once remarked about solo tripping, "All my life people have been telling me you should never travel alone. But it's interesting; I've never been told that by anybody who's ever done it." After all I have read and written on the benefits of venturing solo, Mason's simplicity says it best.

Many cultures have used solitude as a type of initiation into the meaning of life. Natives regard aloneness as a way for shamans to conjure up magic. The Ojibway looked at wilderness solitude with reverence, a place for them to discover their own individual identity as well as to build character. After fasting alone, they believed a vision would grant each brave his guardian angel.

My Ojibway friend, Jim Black, told me of his vision quest. To him it was a time for regeneration, a cleansing of the body and mind, and the realization of nature's powerful magic.

My first solo trip was years ago along the Root River, north of Sault Ste. Marie. I battled loneliness for the first few days, spending each night curled up in the fetal position, wide awake and jumping at the night sounds. But every time I felt spooked, I reminded myself how

Happiness makes up in height for what it lacks in length.
ROBERT FROST

many others had traveled alone before me and gained insight from solitude. That realization marked a turning point in my emotions. Complete loneliness was suddenly transformed into a sense of freedom, an invigorating and exciting awareness of the life around as well as within me. It didn't take long before every little noise that had kept me awake was soon lulling me to sleep.

Apart from the insightful aspects of solo travel there are many other positive points: you can make camp where you want, prepare food pleasing to your taste buds, travel when you think it is necessary, and relax when you believe it to be appropriate.

After an extended solo adventure I think back to my fears. Amazingly enough, what unsettles me most is not the loneliness which at times creeps up, the moment when complete darkness blankets the campsite, or being challenged by foul weather. It is when the trip is over and I am driving away from my place of vision and have to prepare myself mentally for the jam-packed expressway, crowded with thousands of people. More than once I have turned tail on one of the cut-offs, phoned home to let someone know of my altered plans and headed back out into the wilds for a few extra days — alone and content.

Kevin Callan, *Ways of the Wild*

The greatest joy in nature
is the absence of man.
BLISS CARMEN

LEADERSHIP

I then addressed them, by recommending them all to be thankful for their late very narrow escape. I also stated, that the navigation was not impracticable in itself, but from our ignorance of its course; and that our late experience would enable us to pursue our voyage with greater security. I brought to their recollection, that I did not deceive them, and that they were made acquainted with the difficulties and dangers they must expect to encounter, before they engaged to accompany me. I also urged the honour of conquering disasters, and the disgrace that would attend them on their return home, without having attained the object of the expedition. Nor did I fail to mention the courage and resolution which was the peculiar boast of the North men; and that I depended on them, at that moment, for the maintenance of their character. I quieted their apprehension as to the loss of the bullets, by bringing to their recollection that we still had shot from which they might be manufactured. I at the same time acknowledged the difficulty of restoring the wreck of the canoe, but confided in our skill and exertion to put it in such a state as would carry us on to where we might procure bark, and build a new one. In short, my harangue produced the desired effect, and a very general assent appeared to go wherever I should lead the way.

Journals and Letters of Alexander Mackenzie,
entry for Thursday, June 13, 1793, during Mackenzie's
expedition to the Pacific Ocean.

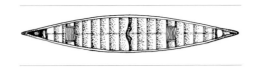

RESPECTING WILDERNESS

WHY WILDERNESS?

Ask the men who have known it and who have made it part of their lives. They might not be able to explain, but your very questions will kindle a light in eyes that have reflected the camp fires of a continent, eyes that have known the glory of dawns and sunsets and nights under the stars. Wilderness to them is real and this they do know; when the pressure becomes more than they can stand, somewhere back of beyond, where roads and steel and towns are still forgotten, they will find release.

Sigurd Olson, in *American Forests*

REQUIEM FOR A RIVER:
DEATH BY HYDRO-ELECTRIC DAMS, 1983

rapper Ray wanted to shoot the Grand Canyon and wanted me to scout Devil's Gorge with him.... We stayed with Trapper Ray for three days. We overnighted at his stage cabin downstream where the Deer River, a knee-deep trout stream gurgling pleasantly over small stones, splashes into the Liard. We ran the Liard to the beginning of the Grand Canyon, floating downstream with the ease of a morsel into a mouth, which suddenly became the enormous open maw of some mad animal, gleaming with spittle and froth. From atop the 150-metre canyon wall we scouted Devil's Gorge — the ten-metre-high waves, opening and closing eddies and whirlpools, standing waves of two, three, and four metres, and dead ahead the headwall. From that height the waves looked like riffles in cake frosting sliding slowly and majestically in the sun.

Farther downstream raged the Rapids of the Drowned, Surrender Island, Hell's Gate: suicidal rapids all. When at last we left, not having run the canyon, we appreciated Trapper Ray's outlook. Why not go out with one last gesture of defiance? Here where he had made his life and swamped a road through jungle, along this river that for him was home and, from our perspective, paradise... all this would soon all be underwater, a huge, shapeless lake "to 2000 feet contour," a swamp.

"Might as well move to Siberia," Ray muttered at the prospect.

Might as well. The winters are no colder there, and the dams are already built.

Thomas York, in *Wild Waters*

WILDERNESS UNDIMINISHED

It is certainly not my intention to convince everybody they should grab a canoe and take to the wilderness. We are all different, and our interests vary. That is how it should be. Some people are content to enjoy the land from the edge of the road or campground. Others are only happy when isolated from the synthetic world by many portages and miles of trackless wilderness. I used to think it was a major tragedy if anyone went through life never having owned a canoe. Now I believe it's only a minor tragedy.

The important thing is for those people who are not wilderness lovers to realize that it's good to have places where modern technology can never intrude — not for the sake of canoeists, but for the sake of the animals that live there. Their well-being should concern us. We wilderness freaks also have to realize, though, that we can't turn the clock back. We can only hope that, at least in certain areas, we can stop the clock. Every day, somewhere, a road is pushed a little farther, penetrating deeper and deeper to provide easy access into wild places. For those who truly love wild places, a road that cuts through a wilderness area diminishes its size by half. For the animal and the plant life, the land has diminished that much more.

I would much prefer to paddle, portage, track, and wade up some unnavigable waterway to the base of a spectacular waterfalls, pitch my camp, and sit there drinking in their beauty, than travel there by road. It isn't the same. The falls you have to work to get to are always the biggest, the best, the most spectacular, even if they aren't as high....

Many times I have been canoeing on a wild, remote river and found a camper truck parked at the water's edge, halfway down. All of a sudden the river doesn't feel so endless anymore. It's a totally irrational feeling, I know, but I'm stuck with it.

Bill Mason, *Path of the Paddle*

Algonquin Recognized, oil on canvas, Jeff Miller

Canoe Irony

The canoeist should know the ironic role of the canoe in the evolving Canadian culture. The canoe was a serious factor in conflict, death, dichotomy and compromise. Despite the canoe's mythological purity as a symbol, it was, in fact, part of the "idea of progress" which led to the continuing destruction of wilderness and the degradation of the environment.

This ironic truth can give us the knowledge and determination to struggle to preserve parts of that natural environment as seen by the early canoeists in Canada. The canoeist should ultimately know that, in Canadian culture, the myth of the canoe as wilderness symbol is more important than the blurred and complex reality. The canoeist should see that an emotional commitment to the preservation of lands approximating wilderness and a year-round concern for our canoeing heritage is more important than a cold, rational and unreflective control of the canoe on a two-week vacation, away from it all. Usually, the vacation canoe trip is followed by a return to the concrete jungle and to participation in the general degeneration of the Canadian environment, all in the name of economic growth and development. Certainly, the canoeist should avoid and reject the use of expressions connoting conflict with the wilderness. We never "conquer" a river or a route, unless societally, we participate in polluting it or ravaging its shoreline. And then, in the long run, it is we who are conquered. It was perhaps fortuitous that on the new Canadian one dollar coin the symbolic voyageur canoe, harbinger of destruction, lost out to the symbolic loon, icon of wilderness. We canoeists should realize we have a special and major responsibility to see that the cry of the loon is never silenced.

Bruce Hodgins, *Canexus*

Spring

We can never have enough of nature. We must be refreshed by the sight of inexhaustible vigor, vast and Titanic features, the sea-coast with its wrecks, the wilderness with its living and its decaying trees, the thundercloud, and the rain which lasts three weeks and produces freshets. We need to witness our own limits transgressed, and some life pasturing freely where we never wander.

Henry David Thoreau, *Walden*

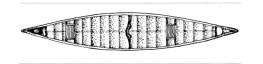

TRIP'S END AND AFTER

MILE 352

As we came around a bend and paddled a few hundred yards up a little creek, we saw the building that marks Mile 352. Immediately we beached our canoes and raced up, each one trying to be the first to see "steel." Soon we came upon the tracks, which stretch for many miles along the sub-Arctic barrens. We had our lunch and began bringing up our canoes and loads to the tracks. About nine o'clock we heard a whistle. Along jerked a freight train, heading south, and at the end was a palatial old pullman, which seemed like the Waldorf Astoria. When the conductor saw our load, he immediately backed the train until a box-car came alongside, into which we loaded our paraphernalia. When that car was full he brought up another, for us to put the rest of the things in. As he said, it was much easier for the engineer to back the train than for us to carry the load. On board the train was a candy dealer, who did a rushing business with us, selling oranges, candy, cookies and other super-delicacies.

John Stern, *To Hudson's Bay by Paddle and Portage*, 1934

LAUNDRY DAY

The voyageurs brought forth all the soiled clothing worn upon the journey, and a general scrubbing took place. Soon the bushes in the vicinity, the branches of trees, and the flat rocks, bore plentiful burdens of gaudy apparel waving in the breeze to dry. Copious baths were next administered to their persons, capped by each man donning the bravest garments of his outfit. Ribbons were braided in their hair, flashy sashes encircled their waists, and moccasins of bewildering beadwork encased their feet. Then, with a dash and wild chorus of boat-song, the oars were plied with quickly-measured stroke. Soon the sharp point of a headland was turned, and the Mission of the White Dog appeared....

M. Robinson, "A Voyage with the Voyageurs," *Appleton's Journal*, 1878

It never fails.
Nature always saves a special treat for trippers heading
out onto a big lake near the end of a trip, especially if
hot showers and warm beds are within reach.
A head wind whips up, rollers fight even minimal
progress, and a steady rain sets in.

ANNE OPTIMIST

The ghosts of canoe trip present flap angrily before us as we taunt them
while drinking down the fiery spirits already captured in our camp cups.

WHAT NEXT?

August 26. The trip had ended in a crashing anticlimax. We were emotionally empty. The delight and sense of achievement we had anticipated so long had not appeared. Nor was there any incentive other than food obsessions that could drag us from the tent in the morning. What was it we had expected I could not remember. A brass band? Welcoming speeches? The keys to the city? Adulation of the raucous multitudes? I did not know. We were left with the vague, rankling impression that we had been cheated of whatever it was we sought. We felt that there should have been, in some fashion or other, a grand and profound conclusion to our long journey, but there was nothing we could pinpoint. It had abruptly ended, expired, died, like the flame of a candle snuffed out between thumb and forefinger.

Our canoe was high and dry. There was no gear to pack, no rapids to wade, no white-capped lake to cross, no agonizing portage awaiting us. We had lost the firm orientation we had while traveling in the wilderness, and had nothing with which to replace it. When we beached our canoe for the final time we lost our purpose in life. Nothing remained, and I did not know what we would do....

Peter Browning, *The Last Wilderness*

THE LAST DAYS

The goal of a wilderness canoe trip should be to collect enough of the wilderness experience to last the whole year. Doing the math is one of the first priorities after the end of the trip. A sad conclusion to the trip when the math shows that not enough has been collected to last the winter. Top that with the knowledge that the last few days have been hurried through and you almost have sacrilege. There are only so many wilderness canoe trips to a lifetime. Every moment of the wilderness experience should be savored and treasured. Including the travel on the limestone [on rivers running north off the Canadian Shield and emptying into Hudson Bay].

Ending the trip hurriedly also risks losing some of the joy so carefully collected during the trip. A full cup is the only way that the winter can be endured. Need all of the joy and challenge and adventure of the current trip to make it to the start time of the next one.

Cities do that to you. Only way out is to fill the cup these last few days by squeezing each moment to the fullest. Concentrate on no place other than here. No time other than now. Till your cup runneth over.

I want to travel carefully these last few days. There is still the chance of a spill.

Greg Went, *Nastawgan*

As I Live

There is rain on the window now, as I write these words, forming silver drops on the branches of a stand of aspens outside, where spring is returning and buds are about to burst into leaf. Beyond the trees is a different landscape that I see, where the great river stirs and coils in its ceaseless flow, the rain patters lightly on the tent and the wind riffles under the tent fly. The two landscapes fold into each other, and I cannot tell you which is the real, the actual; for me, now. For as long as I live, I think, I will inhabit both.

Robert Mead, *Ultimate North*

BIBLIOGRAPHY

Every effort was made to contact the publishers of works cited in this book regarding copyright. In some cases, works were found to be long out of print or their publishers no longer in existence. We regret any errors or omissions and welcome additional information and corrections, which may be supplied care of Boston Mills Press and will be included in all future reprints.

Adams, Arthur T. *The Explorations of Pierre Esprit Radisson*. Minneapolis: Ross and Haines Inc., 1961.

Benedickson, Jamie. *Idleness, Water, and a Canoe: Reflections on Paddling for Pleasure*. Toronto: University of Toronto Press, 1997.

Blake, William Hume. *In a Fishing Country*. Toronto: Macmillan, 1922.

Bolz, Arnold J. *Portage into the Past: By Canoe Along the Minnesota-Ontario Boundary Waters*. Minneapolis: University of Minneapolis Press, 1960.

Burry, Donald. *The Canoe in Canadian Art*. Doctoral Dissertation, University of Alberta, 1993.

Browning, Peter. *The Last Wilderness*. Lafayette, California: Great West Books, 1989.

Callan, Kevin. *The Ways of the Wild*. Peterborough, Ontario: Broadview Press, 1993.

Campbell, Marjorie Wilkins. *The North West Company*. Toronto: Macmillan, 1957.

Carney, Margaret. "I Found It Again — Even in the Buffer Zone." Toronto: *The Globe and Mail*, October 17, 1995.

Champlain, Samuel de. *The Voyages and Explorations of Samuel de Champlain 1604-16*. trans. Annie Nettleton Bourne. New York: Allerton, 1922.

Che-Mun: The Journal of Canadian Wilderness Canoeing. Michael Peake, editor.

Coolican, Denis M. *Canoe Trip Diary*. (Sask, 1955.)

Culpeper, Richard. "Wildwater Technojunkies, Beware." *Nastawga*, Spring 1994.

Davidson, James, and John Rugge. *The Complete Wilderness Paddler*. New York: Alfred A. Knopf, 1975.

Dease, P. W. "Progress of North American Discovery for 1838, Dispatched by the Hudson's Bay Company." Fort Confidence, Great Bear Lake, 1838.

DeVoto, Bernard, ed. *The Journals of Lewis and Clark*. Boston: Houghton Mifflin Co., 1953.

Dickson, James. *Camping in the Muskoka Region: A Story about Algonquin Park*. Ontario Department of Lands and Forests, 1959. First printed in 1886.

Douglas, George M. *Lands Forlorn: The Story of an Expedition to Hearne's Coppermine River*. New York: G. P. Putnam's Sons, 1914.

Downes, P.G. *Sleeping Island*. New York: Coward-McCann, 1943.

Dunraven, Windham Thomas Wyndham-Quin, 4th Earl of. *The Great Divide: Travels in the Upper Yellowstone in the Summer of 1874*. London: Chatto and Windus, 1876.

Fisher, Ronald M. *Still Waters, White Waters*. National Geographic Society, 1975.

Ford, Jesse. "What Did Flies Matter When You Were Free?" in *Rivers Running Free*. Judith Niemi and Barbara Wieser, eds. Copyright Jesse Ford, 1987.

Forgey, William W. *Wilderness Medicine*. 4th Edition. St. Catharines, Ontario: Vanwell Publishing, 1994.

Forgey, William. "Wilderness Medicine." Lecture at Canoeexpo. Toronto. April 9, 1995.

Franks, C.E.S. *The Canoe and Whitewater*. Toronto: University of Toronto Press, 1977.

Fraser, Simon. *Letters and Journals 1806-1808*. W. Kaye Lamb, ed. Toronto: Macmillan, 1960.

Gibbon, John Murray. *The Romance of the Canadian Canoe*. Toronto: Ryerson Press, 1951.

Grey Owl. *The Men of the Last Frontier*. London: Country Life, 1936.

Hartling, R. Neil. *Nahanni: River of Gold, River of Dreams*. Hyde Park, Ontario: Canadian Recreational Canoeing Association, 1993. Neil Hartling runs Nahanni River Adventures, P. O. Box 4869, Whitehorse, Yukon, Y1A 4N6. Phone: (403) 668-3180

Heming, A. "The Abitibi Fur Brigade," excerpts printed in *The Beaver*. Outfit 298: pgs. 32-39, Summer 1967. First published in *Scribner's Magazine*, 1901.

"Historic Canoes and Historic Travels." Twelfth Annual Canoeing and Wilderness Symposium. Toronto. January 31-February 1, 1997.

Hodgins, Bruce. "The Canoe as Chapeau: The Role of the Portage in Canoe Culture." Lecture at Canexus II Conference, Peterborough, May 10, 1996.

Hodgins, Bruce, and Gwynneth Hoyle. *Canoeing North into the Unknown*. Toronto: Natural History Press, 1994.

Hopkins, Gerard Manley. "Inversnaid." *The Poems of Gerard Manley Hopkins*, 4th Edition. Toronto: Oxford University Press, 1967.

Houston, C. Stuart. *To the Arctic by Canoe: The Journal and Paintings of Robert Hood*. Montreal: The Arctic Institute of North America, McGill-Queen's University Press, 1974.

Hubbard, Lucius Lee. *Woods and Lakes of Maine*. Boston: James R. Osgood, 1884.

Hubbard, Mina. *A Woman's Way Through Unknown Labrador*. Breakwater, 1981.

Hurley, Jack, and Jim Spencer. Interview by Don Standfield. March 18, 1997.

Jacobson, Cliff. *Campsite Memories: True Tales from Wild Places*. Merrillville, Indiana: ICS Books, 1994.

_____. *Canoeing Wild Rivers*. Merrillville, Indiana: ICS Books, 1989.

_____. "How to Start a One Match Fire in a Driving Rain," lecture at Canoeexpo. Toronto. April 8, 1995.

Jacobson, Cliff, and Boo Turner. "The Wilberforce Falls Affair," *Canoe*. March 1993.

Jameson, Anna. *Winter Studies and Summer Rambles in Canada*. Toronto: McClelland & Stewart, 1923.

Kerfoot, Justine. *Woman of the Boundary Waters: Canoeing, Guiding, Mushing and Surviving*. Grand Marais, Minnesota: Women's Times Publishing, 1986.

Kesselheim, Alan S. *Water and Sky: Reflections of a Northern Year*. Toronto: Stoddart, 1989.

Klein, Clayton, and Verlen Kruger. *One Incredible Journey*. Fowler, Michigan: Wilderness House Books, 1985.

Klein, Clayton. *Cold Summer Wind*. Fowlerville, Michigan.: Wilderness House Books, 1983.

Keyser, Esther. Interview by Don Standfield. August 21, 1998.

La Vérendrye. *Journals and Letters of Pierre Gaultier de Varennes de La Vérendrye and His Sons*. Toronto: The Champlain Society, 1927.

Leslie, Robert Franklin. *Read the Wild Water: 780 Miles by Canoe Down the Green River*. New York: E. P. Dutton, 1966. Copyright Robert Franklin Leslie. Used by permission of Dutton, a division of Penguin Putnam Inc.

Luste, George. "The Tradition of Wilderness Travel." Lecture at Canexus II Conference. Peterborough. May 11, 1996.

Mackenzie, Alexander. *The Journals and Letters of Sir Alexander Mackenzie*. W. Kaye Lamb, ed. London: Cambridge University Press, 1970.

Madsen, Ken and Graham Wilson. *Rivers of the Yukon: A Paddling Guide*. Whitehorse, Yukon: Primrose Publishing, 1989.

Mason, Bill. *Canoescapes*. Erin, Ontario: Boston Mills Press, 1995.

_____. *Path of the Paddle*. Toronto: Key Porter, 1980.

_____. *Song of the Paddle*. Toronto: Key Porter, 1988.

McGuffin, Gary and Joanie. *Superior: Journeys on an Inland Sea*. Erin, Ontario: Boston Mills Press, 1995.

_____. *Where Rivers Run*. Erin, Ontario: Boston Mills Press, 1999, reprint.

McGuire, Thomas. *99 Days on the Yukon*. Anchorage, Alaska: Northwest Publishing, 1977.

Mead, Robert Douglas *The Canoer's Bible*. New York: Doubleday, 1989.